THE EMERGENCE OF CRACK COCAINE ABUSE

THE EMERGENCE OF CRACK COCAINE ABUSE

EDITH FAIRMAN COOPER

Novinka Books
New York

Senior Editors: Susan Boriotti and Donna Dennis
Coordinating Editor: Tatiana Shohov
Office Manager: Annette Hellinger
Graphics: Wanda Serrano
Editorial Production: Jennifer Vogt, Matthew Kozlowski, and Maya Columbus
Circulation: Ave Maria Gonzalez, Vera Popovich, Luis Aviles, Melissa Diaz,
　　　　　　Nicolas Miro and Jeannie Pappas
Communications and Acquisitions: Serge P. Shohov
Marketing: Cathy DeGregory

Library of Congress Cataloging-in-Publication Data
Available Upon Request

ISBN: 1-59033-512-0

Copyright © 2002 by Novinka Books, An Imprint of
　　　　　Nova Science Publishers, Inc.
　　　　　400 Oser Ave, Suite 1600
　　　　　Hauppauge, New York 11788-3619
　　　　　Tele. 631-231-7269　　　　Fax 631-231-8175
　　　　　e-mail: Novascience@earthlink.net
　　　　　Web Site: http://www.novapublishers.com

Printed in the United States of America

CONTENTS

PREFACE

This book provides background information about the rise of crack cocaine abuse in the United States. It describes the origin of this form of smokable cocaine, warnings that were given about physical and mental health hazards that could result from its abuse, its arrival and spread in the nation, and whether its spread was epidemic. Also, it assesses whether federal government officials were aware of the potential problem before it occurred, and if so, how they responded. In addition, lessons from the crack cocaine phenomenon that could help prevent similar future occurrences involving other illicit drugs are discussed. Individuals involved in formulating drug control policy, and/or interested in learning particularly about the history of the crack cocaine abuse problem in the nation should find this book useful.

Cocaine is the active chemical in the coca plant, primarily grown in South America. In 1970, *California drug dealers reportedly observed people smoking coca paste (a brown powder made from coca leaves) in South America. Trying to duplicate the paste in California, a chemist accidentally discovered cocaine freebase.

In 1974, a recreational smoking of freebase cocaine began in California. Freebasing produced a quicker, more pleasurable "high" than snorting or injecting the drug. Preparing it was time-consuming, expensive and dangerous (ether, a highly flammable liquid was frequently used).

Several warnings about physical and mental health hazards from abuse of smokable cocaine were given by reputable scientists to the medical community, and federal government policymakers, and were published nationally in newspapers and journals. In June 1980, reports that comedian Richard Pryor had a near fatal accident, allegedly while freebasing brought nationwide attention to cocaine abuse. Thereafter, consumer demand grew for drug dealers to prepare freebase in advance for customers.

In 1981, crack cocaine, also called "rock," was available in Los Angeles, San Diego, Houston, and Miami. Crack is a form of cocaine freebase that is easily produced with a nondangerous procedure. Crack reportedly was selling for as little as $3. By 1986, crack had been spread to 28 states and the District of Columbia, primarily by Los Angeles street gangs and Jamaican gangs called "posses," although some commentators question whether drug trafficking was a primary gang activity.

By early 1986, a crack cocaine crisis appeared to be developing among older youth and adults, and escalated by early 1987. A large number of persons 18 years and older suffered medical and psychological problems from crack cocaine abuse. Whether crack's quick spread was an epidemic, however, cannot be proven and is debatable, because of a lack of accurate prevalence data.

By the end of the 1970's, congress was aware of a problem with cocaine and knew about a potential smokable-cocaine crisis. It held many hearings to gather information to assess and define the problem. Landmark legislation was passed in cooperation with the executive branch in an attempt to control crack and other illicit drugs. Several possible approaches to avert future drug crises have arisen from the nation's experience with crack. They include using media public campaigns to educate the public and strengthen society's historical knowledge about past national drug abuse episodes, and encouraging cooperative efforts among law enforcement, public health departments, and local community groups.

Chapter 1

INTRODUCTION

On November 17, 1985, an article appeared in the *New York Times* about a cocaine-abuse treatment program underway in Westchester county, New York.[1] The author mentioned that there was a recent noticeable increase in cocaine use among local teenagers, especially those from middle-class families. Data obtained through a Student Assistance program indicated that in 1984, one-third of the students seen had reported trying cocaine. That was a much larger number of students than the administrators of the program had seen in previous years. In 1985, three teenagers had sought treatment through the program for cocaine dependence that resulted from using a "new form of the drug called 'crack,' or rock-like pieces of prepared 'freebase' (concentrated) cocaine." That news report was the first mention by name of crack cocaine in the major media. Twelve days later, in the November 29, 1985 *New York Times,* another article appeared discussing the "new' drug being sold on New York City streets that was alarming law enforcement officials and rehabilitation experts because of its tendency to hasten abuse, especially among youth.[2]

By 1986, crack cocaine use was considered to be in epidemic proportions in New York City.[3] Furthermore, as a result of the easily marketable value of crack, demand for the drug significantly increased, and by fall of 1986, the 800-COCAINE National Hotline estimated that one

---

[1] Donna Boundy, "Program for Cocaine-Abuse Under Way," *New York Times,* 17 November 1985, sec.11WC, 12.

[2] Jane Gross, "A New, Purified Form of Cocaine Causes Alarm as Abuse Increases," *New York Times,* 29 November 1985, sec.A,1.

[3] Andrew Golob and Bruce D. Johnson, "A Recent decline in Cocaine Use Among Youthful Arrestees in Manhattan, 1987 Through 1993," *American Journal of Public Health* 84 (August 1994): 1250.

million people in the nation used crack.[4] In a short period of time, crack cocaine became a household word that was often equated with crime, violence, and medical problems that sometimes led to death. A derivative of cocaine hydrochloride (cocaine powder), which was an expensive drug once considered by many to be the "safe" and "fashionable" drug of the elite, crack cocaine could be afforded by the elite, the "man-on-the-street," and inner-city community dwellers.

The intensity and apparent suddenness of crack cocaine's widespread use and abuse raise several important questions. Were there warning signs that alerted federal government and public health officials that widespread abuse of this form of cocaine was imminent? How did crack cocaine use and abuse spread nationwide? Was the spread of crack abuse an epidemic in public health terms? What actions were taken by federal government officials to combat the spread of crack abuse? What lessons could be learned and applied from the experience with crack to avoid similar future prominent abuse of other illegal drugs?

This report addresses those questions. It describes cocaine, cocaine freebase, and crack cocaine. It traces the rise of crack cocaine abuse from the earliest know use of smokable cocaine in the nation to the time when crack was considered by some to be a major health problem. It discusses warning signs about the health hazards of smokable cocaine and its potential abuse, the arrival of crack cocaine, and its spread and significant impact on older youth and adults. A brief discussion is provided examining whether federal government officials were aware of a possible smokable cocaine problem before it occurred and if so, how they responded. Also, the report explores lessons that could be applied when considering ways to avoid similar problems in the future involving other illicit drugs. Two appendices provide information about preclinical and clinical studies that were conducted in the 1970's investigating the effects of cocaine powder and smokable cocaine, and a detailed chronology of the emergence and development of crack cocaine abuse in the nation.

---

[4] Gordon Witkin et al., "The Men who Created Crack," *U.S. News and World Report,* 19 August 1991, 51.

Chapter 2

THE ORIGIN OF COCAINE POWDER AND SMOKABLE COCAINE

Crack cocaine is a smokable form of the drug cocaine. Knowledge about cocaine is necessary in order to understand the emergence of crack cocaine use and abuse in the United States. The origin of cocaine, its various routes of administration, and impact on the body are discussed below.

COCAINE POWDER

Cocaine can be traced to the coca plant, which is a shrub that grows in the Andes mountains primarily in Peru and Bolivia, South America. Cocaine is the coca plant's main psychoactive ingredient. The processing of 500 kilograms of coca leaves yields one kilogram of cocaine hydrochloride powder, which is a whit, odorless, crystal-like matter.[1] In 1988, this substance had a retail value on the "illicit street market" that ranged from $75 to $100 per gram, with a drug purity range from 30% to 75%.[2]

Cocaine hydrochloride (its chemical name) is both a local anesthetic and a stimulant to the central nervous system (CNS). It is the only known drug that possesses both or more properties.[3] It directly stimulates the brain and gives the user strong feelings of more alertness and energy.

---

[1] Oakley Ray and Charles Ksir, *Drugs, Society, & Human Behavior,* 7th ed. (St. Louis: Mosby-Year Book, 1996), 135,139.

[2] Arnold M. Washton, *Cocaine Addiction: Treatment, Recovery, and Relapse Prevention,* (New York: W.W. Norton & Com., 1989), 11.

[3] Ibid.

Methods of Administering Cocaine

To produce the stimulating effects of the drug, cocaine users choose one of three methods to self-administer the drug – snorting, injecting, or smoking.

Snorting

The intranasal method is called sorting. Typically, the drug is prepared for snorting by placing cocaine hydrochloride on a mirror or piece of glass, chopping the crystalline matter into a fine consistency with a razor blade, and pushing and separating it into one- or two-inch narrow lines. The user employs either a straw or rolled-up dollar bill to sniff the substance into the nostrils, or puts a small amount into a tiny "coke spoon" and lifts it into the nose to be inhaled.[4] It takes about five minutes or so for the effects of the drug to reach the brain and produce a "high" or euphoric feeling. The high can last from 20 minutes up to two hours depending on the individual.[5] When the high wears off, the user becomes irritable, depresses, and anxious, and begins craving more of the drug. A person can become addicted to cocaine by snorting the drug over a period of years.[6]

Injecting

Cocaine powder is water soluble and can liquified and placed into a syringe for intravenous (IV) injection.[7] The IV cocaine user prepares the drug by placing about 1/8 or ¼ of a gram of cocaine on a spoon, adding water to dissolve it, and then straining the substance through a small mesh strainer. The solution is then drawn into a syringe and injected into a vein. This method takes about 30 to 60 seconds to produce a "high."[8] One analyst stated that it takes only 14 seconds for the drug to reach the brain through IV cocaine use.[9] The high quickly diminishes and in most cases is followed by an intense "crash" producing similar oppressed feelings as when the drug is snorted. These irritable, depressed, and anxious feelings usually foster

---

[4] Ibid.

[5] David Lee, *Cocaine Handbook: An Essential Reference*, (Berkeley, CA: And/Or Press, Inc., 1981),48.

[6] Arnold Washton and Mark S. Gold, "Recent Trends in Cocaine Abuse: A View From the National Hotline, '800-COCAINE'," *Advances in Alcohol and Substance Abuse*, 6 (winter 1986): 38.

[7] Ibid., 16.

[8] Ibid.,17.

[9] Dr. Ronald Siegel, telephone conversation with author, 29 May 1997. Dr. Siegel conducted some of the earliest preclinical research involving smokable freebase cocaine in the United States.

repeated injections to escape the crash and obtain the euphoric feelings once again. These activities can cause addiction as well as psychological and medical after effects.[10] IV cocaine users expose themselves to a high risk of infection from using contaminated needles, as well as contracting serious diseases such s AIDS, or hepatitis.[11]

Smoking

To be smoked, the cocaine powder has to be converted through a chemical process. That procedure involves mixing cocaine powder with an alkali such as sodium hydroxide or ammonia and boiling it with a solvent such as ether.[12] When dried, cocaine crystals of the freed base remained. Those crystals became popularly known as "freebase."[13] During the 1970's and early 1980's, ether (a dangerously volatile liquid) was routinely used as the solvent in performing this chemical procedure.[14] There were five common freebase techniques in California during the previously mentioned time period. They were The California Clean-up Method, The Careful California Method (ether was used in both methods as the solvent), The Baking Soda Method (discussed below), The ammonia Method, and The Spoon Method (ammonia hydroxide was used in both as the solvent).[15]

Most often, users smoked cocaine freebase in commercially available water pipes. In some instances, homemade pipes were constructed. Users placed a small amount of cocaine freebase on the stainless steel screen in the bowl of the pipe. Sometimes three to 15 screens were used to trap the cocaine, which tended to melt when heated, so that it could continue to be vaporized. Heat was applied to the cocaine base from a butane or propane torch, lighter, or matches. The user would then deeply inhale the fumes from the pipe. If several smokers shared the pipe, a larger amount of cocaine freebase was placed on the screen and the pipe would be quickly passed to each user.[16] Technically, cocaine freebase was "inhaled" and not "smoked,"

---

[10] Washton, *Cocaine Addiction*, 17.

[11] Ibid., *Note:* hepatitis is inflammation of the liver (*Stedman's Medical Dictionary*, 25th ed. (Baltimore: Williams & Wilkins, 1990), 704).

[12] Patricia g. Erickson et al., *The Steel Drug: Cocaine and Crack in Perspective*, 2nd ed. (New York: Lexington Books, 1994), 3.

[13] Ronald Siegel, "Cocaine Smoking," *Journal of Psychoactive Drugs: A Multidisciplinary Forum*, 14 (October – December 1982): 312-313.

[14] Washton, *Cocaine Addiction*, 14.

[15] Siegel, "Cocaine Smoking," 312-313.

[16] Ibid., 313.

although the process is referred to as "smoking,"[17] and was popularly called "freebasing."

It takes about 8 to 10 seconds for cocaine to get to the brain when smoking cocaine freebase,[18] or according to another observer, as briefly as six seconds to feel the effects.[19] It has been reported that smoking any drug "delivers higher doses of it into the brain more quickly than any other route of administration."[20] The high received from cocaine freebasing lasts only two to five minutes, followed by a rapid depression and a craving for more of the drug similar to the effects of snoting cocaine powder. With cocaine freebase, however, the symptoms are more severe. In many instances, individuals become rapidly addicted to cocaine freebase and exhibit severe psychiatric reactions such as paranoia, deep depression, and emotional instability. Also, some serious medical problems can be experienced, such as a dramatic increase in blood pressure, heart attacks, strokes, and lung damage.[21]

Crack cocaine is cocaine freebase.[22] During the 1970's in Los Angeles, it was prepared (before the term "crack" was used on the street) by using what was termed "The Baking Soda Method." Cocaine powder was mixed with baking soda and water to form a paste. The mixture then was heated until dried. When dried, the product became a rock-like substance that was broken into chunks and smoked. This method was used at least 10 years before it reached the east coast of the United States, where in the 1980's, it was given the street name "crack"[23] because when heated, the "rocks" (as it was referred to in Los Angeles) made a crackling sound.[24] Many persons in the 1970's drug communities referred to the baking soda method of freebase as "garbage freebase" because of the impurities it contained. It was often discarded as an inferior product.[25]

One drug abuse researcher explained that "crack is converted to the base state *without* removing adulterants.. [it] is not purified cocaine because when it is processed the baking soda remains as a salt and can reduce the purity of

---

[17] M. Perez-Reyes et al, "Free-base Cocaine Smoking," *Clinical Pharmacology and Therapeutics*, 32 (October 1982): 450-460.

[18] Washton, *Cocaine Addiction*, 14.

[19] Siegel, telephone conversation with the scientist, 29 May 1997.

[20] Washton, *Cocaine Addiction*, 14.

[21] Ibid., 16.

[22] Ibid., 14.

[23] Siegel, "Cocaine Smoking," 313.

[24] Witkin et al., "The Men Who Created Crack," 46.

[25] James a. Inciardi, *The War on Drugs II: The Continuing Epic of Heroin, Cocaine, Crack, Crime, AIDS, and Public Policy* (Mountain View, CA:Mayfield, 1992), 111.

90 percent cocaine hydrochloride to as low as 40 percent cocaine... The purity of crack ranges from 40 to 80 percent and generally contains portions of the filler and impurities found in the original cocaine hydrochloride, along with some of the sodium bicarbonate from the processing." A few samples of crack cocaine have been found to have only a 5% to 10% purity range of cocaine hydrochloride which, the researcher determined, probably was the result of poor processing.[26]

How this "garbage freebase" became nationally visible is discussed below by recounting the earliest known use of smokable cocaine in the United States to the time when crack abuse widely increased.

THE EVOLUTION OF SMOKABLE COCAINE TO SOCIAL-RECREATIONAL USE

In the early 1970's in Peru, it was popular for drug users to process cocaine into a smokable form by soaking, mixing, and mashing coca leaves in kerosene, gasoline, or sulfuric acid. After the liquid was removed and the substance dried, a gray-white or brown powder remained that was called coca paste or *base* (pronounced *bah-say* in Spanish). [27] The powder was often alternated in layers with tobacco in hand-rolled cigarettes and smoked. Typically, coca paste was smoked straight or in cigarettes mixed with either tobacco or marijuana.[28] The paste could be made into cocaine hydrochloride, which is the most common form of pure cocaine.[29]

In 1970, California drug dealers, while visiting South America, reportedly observed people smoking coca paste.[30] The American drug dealers used the English word "base" rather than the Spanish *base* to refer to this form of cocaine smoking. By inhaling deeply, one dealer later reported,

[26] James A. Inciardi, "Crack-Cocaine in Miami," in *The Epidemiology of Cocaine Use and Abuse,* ed. Susan Schober and Charles Schade, NIDA research Monograph 110, Department of Health and Human Services, Public Health Service, Alcohol, Drug Abuse and Mental Health Administration, National Institute on Drug Abuse (1991), 265.

[27] William A. McKim, *Drugs and Behavior: An Introduction to Behavioral Pharmacology,* 2nd ed. (Englewood Cliffs, New Jersey: Prentice Hall, 1991), 206.

[28] James A. Inciardi, "Crack-Cocaine in Miami," 264.

[29] Ray and Ksir, Drugs, *Society, & Human Behavior,* 139.

[30] Siegel, "Cocaine Smoking," 288. The drug dealers were unidentified.

smoked *base* produced euphoric feelings similar to those experienced when dissolving cocaine powder in water and using it intravenously.[31]

In 1972, after returning to the United States, one drug dealer wanted to make his own *base,* and contacted a chemist friend for assistance. Probably due to linguistic confusion with the word "base" and the Spanish pronunciation for *base,* the chemist accidentally discovered what became known as cocaine "freebase."[32] He located the term "base" in the Merck Index (an encyclopedia of chemicals, drugs, and biologicals) and found that the cocaine alkaloid could be freed from the hydrochloride salt to yield cocaine as the base. To perform that chemical process, he used cocaine powder, baking soda, and ether, that yielded an end product of base in the form of tiny, smokable, crystalline chunks or "rocks." Thinking he had duplicated the *base* (i.e., the coca paste smoked in South America), the chemist had in reality discovered cocaine freebase.[33]

Drug dealers, referred to as "chefs," prepared their own "original" form of what they assumed was the South American *base.*[34] Cocaine freebase was chemically different from the *base* smoked in South America. It was a purer or more concentrated form of cocaine for smoking than coca paste because it did not contain cocaine alkaloids or other residues from the leaf extractions.

In the 1970's, prior to the arrival of crack, cocaine use was most often associated with the wealthy, privileged, and drug dealers. This association was considered to be part myth and part reality. The processing of cocaine freebase required access to a large amount of cocaine, which confined its use to the affluent. [35] One puff, according to a Washington D.C. police detective in a 1979 article, could cost as much as $100 to $200. It was very expensive to freebase, i.e., to smoke pure cocaine. "three or four companions," he observed, "smoking coke together can burn up several thousand dollars' worth of the drug in one session."[36]

---

[31] Ibid. Also, Donald R. Wesson, David E. Smith, and Susan C. Steffens, *Crack and Ice: Treating Smokable Stimulant Abuse,* (Center City, Minnesota: Hazelton Foundation, 1992), 21.

[32] Ibid.

[33] Ibid.

[34] Siegel, "Cocaine Smoking," 228. Also, Siegel, telephone conversation with author, 29 May 1997.

[35] Ronald Siegel, "Cocaine and the Privileged Class: A Review of Historical and Contemporary Images," *Advances in Alcohol & Substance Abuse* 4 (Winter 1984): 37, 46.

[36] "Coke Burns Up Dollars," *The U.S. Journal of Drug and Alcohol Dependence* 3 (November 1979): 4.

Freebasing became popular in Hollywood. There was a widespread distribution in California of "underground press"[37] handbooks explaining ways to prepare cocaine freebase. As a result, many drug users already were familiar with the various methods used when social-recreational smoking of the drug began in 1974.[38] Initially, users employed the same method of smoking cocaine freebase as was used in smoking coca paste in South America – i.e., removing tobacco from a commercial cigarette and refilling it with alternate layers of cocaine freebase and tobacco. About one gram of the drug was contained in each cigarette. Two or three people smoked the cigarette over an average four-hour period. Users experienced an intense euphoria that they compared with the effects of intravenous cocaine use.[39] By the mid-to-late 1970's, however, cocaine smoking was supported by a growing drug paraphernalia industry that marketed pipes, chemicals, and extraction kits used for freebasing.[40] Also, instructions of various ways to prepare freebase were contained in the extraction kits.

Ronald K. Siegel, a scientific researcher and faculty member in the Department of Psychiatry and Biobehavioral Sciences at the School of Medicine of the University of California, Los Angeles (UCLA), reported that some users modified the basic smoking technique by inhaling the smoke from the water pipe, then exhaling it into a balloon and reinhaling the smoke, to get the most usage out of the available smoke. Others recovered smokable material from the pipe by scraping the glass stem of the pipe and the screens in the bowl of the pipe. Furthermore, there were some users who felt that the best cocaine freebase was that recycled from the water in the pipe.[41]

By 1980, according to one source, experts believed between 10% and 20% of all cocaine users employing the various preparation methods, were doing freebase exclusively.[42] The danger inherent to the processing when using ether was dramatically revealed on June 9, 1980, when it was reported that comedian Richard Pryor accidentally set himself on fire, allegedly while freebasing. Thereafter, perhaps in part because of the attention that Pryor's

---

[37] The counterculture, alternative or "underground" press emerged in the nation around the mid-1960's, publishing books, newspapers, magazines, comics, etc. Two such publications are *High Times* and *HiLife*. A 1973 underground press publication was entitled *Basic Drug Manufacture.*

[38] Siegel defined *social recreational* as nonmedical drug use in social settings, i.e., among friends or acquaintances who considered it acceptable and pleasurable and wanted to share the experience.

[39] R.K. Siegel et al, "Cocaine Self-Administration in Monkeys by Chewing and Smoking," *Pharmacology Biochemistry & Behavior,* April 1976, 464.

[40] Witkin et al, "The Men Who Created Crack," 46.

[41] Siegel, "Cocaine Smoking," 313-314.

[42] Ibid.

accident received, freebase users started insisting that drug dealers prepare the product for customers in advance.[43]

In the early 1980's, when the baking soda method of preparing cocaine freebase was "discovered" and called crack, it was packaged in small, clear vials and sold on the streets. A vial contained one to three rocks of crack and cost from $3 to $20 or more, depending on the size and number of rocks in the vials.[44] Through the manufacture of crack, this form of freebase was made more readily accessible to users of all socioeconomic backgrounds.[45] Major centers of crack dealing, however, most often occurred in inner-city neighborhoods.[46]

Crack cocaine probably became popular because it was easily and safely manufactured: it was inexpensive and affordable: and it produced rapid, intense feelings of well-being, causing users quickly to crave for more. Drug dealers readily recognized crack's market potential and eagerly capitalized on the drug, which almost immediately generated great demand.

Before crack cocaine appeared, ample warnings and warning signs of physical and mental health hazards related to smokable cocaine use were evident and documented. Some of these occurrences are discussed below.

---

[43] Michael Massing, "Crack's Destructive Sprint Across America," *New York Times Magazine*, 1 October 1989, 41.

[44] Arnold M. Washton and Donna Boundy, *Cocaine and Crack: What You Need to Know* (Hillside, New Jersey, 1989), 21.

[45] See p. 15, "The Arrival of Crack Cocaine Use in the Nation," for an explanation regarding why crack was cheaper to manufacture than the purer form of cocaine freebase used by the more affluent before 1981.

[46] Department of Justice, Drug Enforcement Administration, *Crack Cocaine: Overview 1989*, coordinated by John W. Featherly and Eddie B. Hill, (Washington, D.C.: 1989), 13.

Chapter 3

WARNING SIGNS OF POSSIBLE HARM FROM COCAINE FREEBASE ABUSE

During most of the 1970's, cocaine was popular because it was considered to be the "ideal" drug – i.e., it was convenient to use, supposedly had very few side effects, and consequently, was considered to be very safe.[1] That image as the safe drug of choice for the privileged was about to change. Warnings and warning signs about possible physical and mental hazards related to smokable cocaine abuse occurred with hospital admissions in 1974 and 1981, with alerts given to the national medical community, international medical and sociological professionals, and to the U.S. Congress in 1979. Various newspaper and journal articles expressed concerns in the early 1980's and a 1980 cocaine freebasing incident drew national attention to the practice and hazards involved in smoking cocaine. Those occurrences are discussed below.

HOSPITAL ADMISSIONS[2]

A notable early warning sign of possible future occurrences of cocaine freebase-related problems occurred in 1974 with the first record in the nation of a person admitted to a hospital emergency room with a cocaine freebase-

---

[1] Ronald K. Siegel, "Cocaine: Recreational Use and Intoxication," in *Cocaine: 1977*, ed. Robert C. Peterson and Richard C. Stillman, NIDA Research Monograph 13, Department of Health, Education, and Welfare, Public Health Service, Alcohol, Drug Abuse, and Mental Health Administration, National Institute on Drug Abuse (1977), 127.

[2] Other smokable cocaine-related hospital admissions might have occurred in the nation. These three incidents are drawn from the medical literature.

related concern. The situation resulted from the person's fright and panic reaction after his first episode of freebasing.[3] The 31-year-old male was admitted to the UCLA Hospital emergency room. He had heard about the smoking of *base* in South America and decided to try what he believed was *base*. Consequently, he smoked 100 mg of cocaine freebase in a cigarette that did not contain tobacco. Immediately he experienced an intense euphoria followed by nervousness, anxiety, shaking and breathing difficulties. Upon admission to the emergency room, he was diagnosed as having delirium, Cheyne-Stokes respiration (which is the first phase of respiratory collapse), and a panic reaction due to extreme cocaine intoxication.[4] This incident was believed to be the result of overstimulation. It was not life-threatening, and no treatment was necessary.[5]

In 1981, Roger D. Weiss and his colleagues at McLean Hospital in Belmont, MA, Massachusetts General hospital, and Harvard Medical School in Boston, reported results after testing two patients who had been admitted to McLean Hospital for drug abuse treatment.[6] One person was a female chronic cocaine abuser who had been an intranasal user but had recently switched to smoking cocaine freebase. Previously, she had smoked marijuana, taken LSD several times, and PCP once. She complained of a morning cough that produced white sputum. The other patient was a male chronic abuser of cocaine, marijuana, and heroin. He had regularly injected heroin, smoked marijuana, and intermittently snorted and injected cocaine. He began freebasing cocaine about six months before his hospital admission. He complained of tenderness on the right side of his abdomen.

Extensive pulmonary function tests were done at Massachusetts general hospital on both patients after they had been drug-free for a minimum of two weeks. The doctors found that lung damage related to the gas exchange surface of the lungs had occurred in both patients. This meant that because of their smokable cocaine abuse, neither patient was getting sufficient oxygen into the blood vessels in their lungs.[7] These test results clinically proved that smokable cocaine could cause lung damage.

---

[3] Siegel, telephone conversation with author, 29 May 1997.

[4] Siegel, "Cocaine Smoking," 289.

[5] Siegel, telephone conversation with author, 29 May 1997.

[6] Roger D. Weiss et al, "Pulmonary Dysfunction in Cocaine Smokers," *American Journal of Psychiatry* 138 (August 1981): 1110-1112.

[7] Roger D. Weiss, McLean Hospital, Belmont, MA, telephone conversation with author, 28 January 1998.

Those three hospital admissions were significant indicators that smokable cocaine was not a safe recreational drug, and its abuse could result in serious mental and physical damage.

MEDICAL COMMUNITY ALERTED

In 1979, the first clinical warning that the practice of smoking cocaine freebase could cause health problems appeared in the February 15, 1979 issue of *The New England Journal of Medicine*. In a letter to the editor, Dr. Siegel expressed concern about health hazards related to smoking cocaine. The concern was based on preclinical and clinical research that he and other scientists had conducted (see appendix 1). Unlike the effects of intranasal use of cocaine powder, cocaine freebasing often caused mydriasis (excessive dilation of the pupil of the eye), anorexia, hyperactivity, insomnia, weight loss, and rapid pulse. In addition, he state that, depending on an individual's personality and the dose of cocaine smoked, a person also could experience manic-like euphoria, depressive-like dysphoria (a state of unhappiness), or schizophrenic-like paranoid psychosis (an irrational suspiciousness and distrustfulness of others).

He suggested that physicians should consider the role of cocaine smoking when scrutinizing possible causes of certain medical complaints, if a patient mentioned the above symptoms.[8]

INTER-AMERICAN SEMINAR ON MEDICAL AND SOCIOLOGICAL ASPECTS OF COCA AND COCAINE

In July 1979, several scientists from North and South America who conducted cocaine-related research assembled at the Inter-American Seminar on Medical and Sociological Aspects of Coca and Cocaine held in Lima, Peru. The purpose of the conference was twofold – to review historical studies about the use of the coca plant and its derivatives, as well as to present biochemical reports examining the plant's alkaloids[9] and other compounds, and to determine the effects of coca leaf chewing, coca paste

---

[8] Ronald K. Seigel, "Cocaine Smoking" [Letter to The Editor], *The New England Journal of Medicine* 300 (15 February 1979): 373.

[9] The alkaloid is the vegetable base of a plant. *Stedman's Medical Dictionary*, 25th ed. (Baltimore: Williams and Wilkins, 1990), 44.

smoking, and intranasal use and intravenous injections of cocaine hydrochloride.[10]

Sponsored by the Pan American Health Organization and organized by the Health Department of the Ministry of the Interior of Peru under the leadership of Dr. Raul Jeri, conference delegates arrived at some tentative conclusions. Two of them were related to cocaine smoking, particularly coca paste smoking. They found that coca paste smoking was potentially harmful because of the cocaine, and that it should be investigated further with experimental models.[11]

Several U.S. scientists were allowed to examine and question hospitalized Peruvian patients who suffered from disorders related to smoking coca paste. The observers from Yale University, the National Institute on Drug Abuse (NIDA), the White House, and the Department of State shared their concerns about this growing problem in South America when they returned to the United States.[12] The significance of this conference was expressed by an attendee, Dr. Robert Byck, a physician, psychiatrist, clinical pharmacologist, and Professor of Psychiatry and Pharmacology at Yale University, in testimony about smokable cocaine at 1979 hearings before the U.S. House Select Committee on Narcotics Abuse and Control.

The U.S. Congress Alerted

In 1979, warnings about possible health hazards related to smokable cocaine abuse were just beginning to surface and were not yet problems of broad national concern. Interest in the availability, abuse, and popularity of cocaine powder in the nation, however, had been brought to the attention of some Members of Congress. With a reported 19 metric tons of cocaine being illegally brought into the United States in 1978, the House Select Committee on Narcotics Abuse and Control held three days of hearings in 1979, two in July and one in October, to investigate cocaine and provide the public with sound and clear information about the drug and the health implications of its use.[13] The Select Committee was the only congressional forum with a broad

---

[10] *Cocaine 1980: Proceedings of the Interamerican Seminar on Medical and Sociological Aspects of Coca and Cocaine,* ed. F.R. Jeri, (Lima, Peru: Pacific Press, 1980), xiii.

[11] Ibid., xiii-xiv.

[12] Siegel, "Cocaine Smoking," 293.

[13] House Select Committee on Narcotics Abuse and Control, *Cocaine: A Major Drug Issue of the Seventies: Hearings,* 96th Cong., 1st Sess., 24, 26 July, 10 October 1979, 1.

authority for oversight into drug abuse problems.[14] Through the testimony of various witnesses at the July hearings, not only were concerns voiced about cocaine powder, but warnings emerged about a smokable form of cocaine. Robert C. Petersen, Ph.D., Assistant Director of the Division of Research at NIDA, testified at the first day of hearings. NIDA was the primary federal government public health agency responsible for reducing the demand for illicit drugs. Also, it sponsored and conducted research on the causes and effects of drug abuse and explored ways to develop effective treatment and prevention efforts to direct public and private program development and planning.[15] Dr. Petersen provided an overview about cocaine abuse based upon NIDA's 1977 cocaine study.[16] During his testimony, he mentioned the concern about cocaine smoking that initially had been confined to Latin America, but had recently been reported to be occurring in the United States. He informed the select committee that kits available through the drug paraphernalia industry enabled users to convert cocaine powder into cocaine freebase. Also, he mentioned the findings of one researcher who reported that the practice of smoking cocaine base began in California and had spread to Nevada, Colorado, New York, South Carolina, and Florida.

Dr. Petersen explained, as would Dr. Robert Byck on the following day, that smoking cocaine was more serious than "snorting" because of its ability to cause a psychological dependency and produce more serious psychological symptoms. Furthermore, he testified that NIDA was considering the desirability of a vigorous multimedia prevention campaign to discourage cocaine smoking and educate users about the drug's potential health hazards when used in that manner. In addition, he stated that NIDA was planning extensive research to examine this new pattern of cocaine use.[17]

At the end of his testimony, Petersen prophetically warned of a harmful potential public abuse of the drug when he stated that, "At present, we are confronted with a drug which has a moderately high potential for abuse, *were it more readily available at much lower cost.*" (emphasis added) Also, he said, "cocaine's present high cost and limited availability have undoubtedly contributed much to the relatively benign public health picture

---

[14] House Select Committee on Narcotics Abuse and Control, *Federal Drug Strategy: Prospects for the 1980's: Hearing,* 96th Cong., 2nd Sess., 23 September 1980, 2.

[15] Susan B. Lachter and Avraham Forman, "Drug Abuse in the United States," in *Communication Campaigns About Drugs: Government, Media, and the Public,* ed. Pamela J. Shoemaker (Hillsdale, New Jersey: Lawrence Erlbaum Associates, 1989), 7-8.

[16] *Cocaine: 1977,* ed. Petersen and Stillman, NIDA Research Monograph 13.

presently seen. Because it has not posed a serious public health threat at current levels of use, NIDA's research investment has remained modest over the past 4 years, less than $1 million per year, to support about 40 projects per year investigating this drug." [18]

On the second day of hearings, Dr. Robert Byck also cautioned the Select Committee about the potential drug abuse problem caused by smoking cocaine. This concern related to results of his research on coca paste smoking, and on information reported to him by Dr. Raul Jeri (of the University of San Marcos in Peru) about the impact of coca paste smoking on Peruvian patients. [19] Dr. Byck explained that cocaine smoking was an extremely dangerous habit because it produced an initial euphoric feeling that users tried to duplicate by repeatedly taking the drug. He voiced his concern about cocaine freebase smoking, which was not yet a serious problem in this country.[20] He warned the Select Committee of his concern about this new "smoking" route of administration of cocaine, and that, although not widespread, it could become a serious new problem. Cocaine, he related, could suddenly become a dangerous drug when used in this manner.[21] Furthermore, Dr. Byck warned that smokable cocaine was addictive, and it was on drug that attention should be focused upon.

As a preventative measure to eliminate the chance of cocaine freebase becoming a drug epidemic in the nation, he suggested that the federal government initiate an educational campaign about such drug use.[22] He recommended three preventative measures – find out about the drug, create some type of collaboration with the media, and report what happens when the drug itself is used (i.e., that people could become addicted) to head off potentially widespread use.[23] In his written testimony to the Select Committee, he stressed that, "We do not yet have an epidemic of free base or coca paste smoking in the United States. The possibility is strong that this might occur ... cocaine smoking represents a serious health hazard." [24]

Dr. Byck emphasized the need for research to examine the dangers of smoking cocaine and for education to prevent a drug epidemic. Near the end of his written testimony, however, he observed that the country probably

---

[17] House Select Committee, *Cocaine: A Major Drug Issue of the Seventies*, 16.

[18] Ibid., 17.

[19] Ibid., 62.

[20] Ibid.

[21] Ibid., 62.

[22] Ibid., 63.

[23] Ibid.

[24] Ibid., 91.

could not wait a long time for research or a planned educational campaign to get underway. He felt that a dangerous drug abuse phenomenon was upon the nation, and rapid action should be taken. He suggested that a collaborative research effort between U.S. scientists and similar experts in South America might be a course to take to investigate the effects of the drug, and the reasons why people use drugs in certain patterns. In addition, he felt that it was equally important that legislators, scientists, educators, and the press meet to openly discuss how to deal more effectively with drug abuse problems.[25] How members of the Select Committee responded to address the concern is discussed below.

PRESS COVERAGE ABOUT THE HAZARDS OF USING COCAINE FREEBASE

Warning signs of potential abuse and harm that could occur from freebasing were not reported in the press until 1979 and thereafter, following the issuance of the first clinical warning to the medical community. Prior to that time, cocaine freebasing was conveyed benignly in the press as a 'safe' recreational drug alternative to cocaine powder. By the end of 1979, however, that belief was being publicly discounted.

From January through the end of May 1980, warnings about cocaine freebasing were reported in various journal and newspaper articles throughout the nation. One article that appeared in the January issue of the *Medical Tribune* alerted the public about a possible epidemic of cocaine smoking.[26] The author quoted warnings from Dr. Byck and Dr. Donald Wesson, a psychiatrist in Berkeley, California, formerly associated with the Haight-Ashbury Free Clinic, who had treated patients who smoked cocaine freebase. An article in the May issue of *Rolling Stone* magazine entitled, "FREEBASE: A Treacherous Obsession," reported freebase to be "…the top-of-the-line model of the Cadillac of drugs." The writer stated that the drug was very popular in Hollywood and its use was rumored to be rampant among superstar performers and executives. The author cautioned, however, that freebasing seemed to be much more dangerous than snorting cocaine. Medical-clinical personnel had observed a number of freebase-related problems from persons complaining of paranoid feelings and sometimes near

---

[25] Ibid., 92.

[26] Susan Allport, "Epidemic of Cocaine Smoking Seen," *Medical Tribune,* January 1980. This article also appeared in *Hospital Tribune,* March 1980.

overdoses. Freebase was not a problem on the street, the author noted, because of the cost. [27]

THE RICHARD PRYOR INCIDENT

On June 9, 1980, national attention was brought to cocaine freebasing when comedian Richard Pryor suffered third degree burns over the upper half of his body allegedly while using a butane torch to heat cocaine freebase he had prepared with ether. Later, he denied that drugs were involved in the incident, but admitted that he had been freebasing three days straight prior to the accident.[28] In a 1986 television interview with Barbara Walters, Pryor claimed that the fire was the result of a suicide attempt because he could not overcome his freebase addiction.[29] Whatever the facts of the incident, this occurrence led to a significant number of newspaper headlines across the country relating the dangers of cocaine freebasing to the general public.

Siegel lists several headlines that appeared after the Pryor incident about the dangers of this new drug practice. Headlines included the *Los Angeles Herald Examiner,* June 11, 1980, "'Free Base': What It Is and Why It's Dangerous"; the *Philadelphia Daily News,* June 12, 1980, "Freebasing: A Highly Dangerous High"; the *Chicago Tribune,* June 12, 1980, "Medic Warns of Use of Costly 'Free Base'"; and *People Weekly,* June 30, 1980, "Richard Pryor's Tragic Accident Spotlights a Dangerous Drug Craze: 'Freebasing'." [30] In response to public inquiries NIDA issued a publication, *NIDA Capsules,* through its Press Office explaining the cocaine freebase phenomenon.[31]

The Pryor incident appears to have greatly contributed to the change in the image of cocaine use. Television news stories featured freebase paraphernalia as reports about the occurrence and the "new" drug practice were told. Sales in cocaine freebase kits and chemicals for freebase preparation were reported to have declined for two weeks following the Pryor accident. Subsequently, such sales began to climb once again.[32] Possibly due in part to the attention that Pryor's accident received, one writer

---

[27] Charles Perry, "FREEBASE: A Treacherous Obsession," *Rolling Stone*, May 1, 1980, 43.

[28] Fred Robbins and David Ragan, *Richard Pryor: This Cat's Got 9 Lives* (New York: Delilah books, 1982), 13.

[29] Inciardi, *The War on Drugs II,* 109.

[30] Siegel, "Cocaine Smoking," 296-297.

[31] "Cocaine freebase," *NIDA Capsules,* C80-6, June 1980.

[32] Seigel, "Cocaine Smoking," 297.

surmised that user demand increased for dealers to convert cocaine powder to freebase in advance, to avoid the danger and hassle associated with preparing the product.[33]

[33] Massing, "Crack's Destructive Sprint Across America," 41.

Chapter 4

THE ARRIVAL OF CRACK COCAINE
USE IN THE NATION

In 1985, the word "crack" was first introduced into the "street" drug vocabulary. As far as can be ascertained, the word was first used in New York City.[1] Crack, which, as previously discussed, is produced through the baking soda method of processing cocaine powder into smokable freebase form, had been in use primarily in the Los Angeles area since 1974. It was known by other names, such as "rock" and "base," and also was referred to by some as "garbage freebase".

There are several accounts about how the transition occurred in cocaine smoking from freebase use and abuse allegedly among the affluent, to crack cocaine use and abuse among the common populace. One explanation, put forward by Michael R. Aldrich,[2] is that when U.S. Drug Enforcement Administration (DEA) officials pressured officials in Colombia, South America to outlaw ether, used to convert cocaine hydrochloride into cocaine freebase, major drug labs switched to the Caribbean. There chemists used the baking soda process to make freebase, and introduced "baking soda base" to Miami and New York. Crack processing did not remove the impurities that were in the original cocaine. Those impurities could include some baking soda remaining in the product, dirt, insects, or any other adulterants that dealers might want to include to give the product more weight. Because of the impurities, dealers could sell the vials, which contained one to three

---

[1] Ronald Seigel, "Repeating Cycles of Cocaine Use and Abuse," in *Treating Drug Problems,* vol. 2, ed. Dean R. Gerstein and Herrick J. Harwood (Washington, National Academy Press, 1992), 299.

rocks, from $3 to $20 dollars each (depending on the size and number of rocks in the vials) and double their money because of the lower unit price for cocaine powder. Cocaine freebase (a purer cocaine substance) was expensive and could cost as much as $75 to $100 per gram of cocaine powder to prepare the substance.

Author and researcher Terry Williams presents a different account in his book, *The Cocaine Kids.*[3] He reported that in 1978, cocaine "importers," fearing that cocaine prices would decline in New York City because they had stockpiled the drug, decided to keep demand up by including a small quantity of freebase in their shipments. They encouraged drug dealers to urge users to experiment with the "new" product. Freebase did not catch on at first because it was so expensive and was restricted to a small group of customers. By 1980 or 1981, cocaine freebase became popular in New York City. By 1983, however, there was an oversupply of cocaine in Peru, Bolivia, and Chile, which led those countries to cut their prices. At lower prices, demand grew rapidly and exceeded the supply. A new product – crack – was then introduced that would allow dealers to expand the market and attract a new "class of consumers." By 1984 or 1985, only a few customers requested powdered cocaine.

Another version of crack's beginnings in the United States was that someone from the Bahamas shared knowledge about crack use and its production with U.S. drug dealers.[4] In 1979, cocaine freebasing began in the Bahamas and slowly grew in momentum. By fall 1983, crack abuse was very prominent in the Bahamas. An oversupply of cocaine significantly reduced street costs, and simultaneously, drug dealers switched from "pushing" cocaine powder to selling only crack, which was referred to as "rock."[5] The dealers knew that users would become easily addicted to rock and repeatedly return for more. According to Dr. James Jekel, a Yale University Medical school Epidemiologist who worked with Dr. David Allen, a leading drug-abuse expert practicing in the Bahamas at that time, the switch was a marketing move for profit by the drug dealers. They knew that rock could be safely and quickly made in a kitchen, and by selling this product only, the demand would increase.[6] This move resulted in an epidemic of rock in the

---

[2] Michael R. Aldrich, "Crack (Garbage Freebase)," in David Lee, *Cocaine Handbook: An Essential Reference,* Revised ed. (No city: What If?, 1983), 192.

[3] Terry Williams, *The Cocaine Kids: The Inside Story of a Teenage Drug Ring* (Reading, MA, 1989), 6-7.

[4] Jill Jonnes, *Hep-Cats, Narcs, and Pipe Dreams: A History of America's Romance With Illegal Drugs* (New York: Scribner, 1996), 371.

[5] Witkin et al, "The Men Who Created Crack," 47.

[6] James Jekel, telephone conversation with author, 4 June 1997.

Bahamas. Individuals who had been to either the Bahamas or other Caribbean islands and learned how to prepare crack took that knowledge with them when they migrated to Miami or Los Angeles.[7]

Concerned that crack could become a problem in the United States, Drs. Allen and Jerkel alerted the Yale University Medical School faculty and the people in the surrounding community. The head of the Fairfield County, Connecticut drug program listened, believed such a problem could arise, and made preparations to address the situation.[8] Also, Drs. Jekel and Allen tried to warn a wider audience about this concern, one source reports, but no one else seemed to be alarmed.[9]

The transition from cocaine freebase to crack in the Los Angeles area occurred in another manner, according to Gordon Witkin in his article, "the Men Who Created Crack." In his report, there was a product that was introduced after freebase became popular and before crack became prominent in Los Angeles. As early as 1978, he stated, drug addicts revealed that there was a process catching on called "smearing" or "pasting," which used the baking soda formula (see p. 5). Instead of letting the drug mixture solidify into a "rock," preparers would pour it onto a mirror, take a finger, smear it, and smoke it when dried. The product, the addicts contended, was the transitional product between freebase and crack.. In 1980, Witkin stated, crack made its debut in Los Angeles basically because it was a faster and easier method for drug addicts to get "high." Furthermore, due to that transition, by 1982, Los Angeles hospital emergency room personnel reported the nation's most notable increase in cocaine overdoses, which they attributed to the change in the way the drug was administered – from snorting to injecting to freebasing. By early 1983, the *Los Angeles Sentinel,* a community paper in the predominately black south-central neighborhood, reported a problem with "rock" houses, which were places used for dealing crack.[10]

A controversial version of how crack cocaine became prominent in Los Angeles, particularly in the south-central neighborhood (and eventually throughout the nation) was reported in a series of articles that appeared in the August 18-20, 1996 *San Jose (California) Mercury News* by one of its staff writers, Gary Webb. A *Mercury News* investigation found that "For the

---

[7] Jonnes, "Hep-Cats, Narcs, and Pipe Dreams," 372.

[8] CRS attempted to locate John Higgins-Biddle, the former head of the Fairfield County drug program, to ascertain the procedures he followed to prepare for the possible problem with crack but was unsuccessful.

[9] Witkin et al, "The Men Who Created Crack," 48.

[10] Ibid.

better part of a decade, a San Francisco Bay Area drug ring sold tons of cocaine to the Crips and Bloods street gangs of Los Angeles and funneled millions in drug profits to a Latin American guerilla army run by the U.S. Central Intelligence Agency."[11] Webb reported that one of the main "players" in the drug transactions was Ricky Donnell Ross, a teenage south-central Los Angeles drug dealer.

According to this account, "Freeway" Ricky Ross, as he was called, received large amount of cocaine from Oscar Darillo Blandon Reyes, drug dealer and one of the top California civilian leaders of an anticommunist guerilla army called the Nicaraguan democratic force (Fuerza Democratica Nicaraguense or FDN), also known as "The Contras."[12] Freeway Ricky, Webb contended, turned the cocaine powder into crack and sold it wholesale to "the Crips and Bloods," and to other gangs throughout the country. Furthermore, Webb stated, the Los Angeles gangs used their enormous cocaine profits to arm themselves with automatic weapons and spread crack across the nation (discussed further on pp. 20-25).[13]

In contrast to the Webb account, an October 20, 1996 article in *The Seattle Times* reported that a *Los Angeles Times* investigation found that "the explosion of cheap, smokable cocaine in the 1980s was a uniquely egalitarian phenomenon that lent itself more to makeshift mom-and-pop operations than to the sinister hand of a government-sanctioned plot."[14] The article stated that although it was unclear what, if anything, the U.S. government knew about the drug trade, it was clear that "Cocaine was flowing from Colombia into Los Angeles long before the Nicaraguan trafficker arrived on the scene ..."[15] "The rise of crack," the author concluded, "was driven by a broad array of factors – a worldwide glut of powder cocaine, shifting tastes among addicts, and the entrepreneurial moxie of the inner-city hustlers who marketed it."[16] Also, the authors noted that the executive Editor of the *San Jose Mercury News* later acknowledged that he

---

[11] Gary Webb, "America's 'Crack' Plague Has Roots in Nicaragua War: Columbia-San Francisco Bay Area Drug Pipeline Helped Finance CIA-Backed Contras," August 18, 1996, in *Dark Alliance: The Story behind the Crack Explosion*, [http://www.sjmercury.com/drugs], October 1, 1996.

[12] Gary Webb, "Drug King Free, But Black Aide Sits in Jail: How Cheap Cocaine Became the Scourge of the Inner City," *The Seattle Times – Today's Top Stories, National News*, [http://www.seattletimes.com/extra/browse/html/altdrug_082396.html], 23 August 1996.

[13] Gary Webb, "America's 'Crack' Plague Has Roots in Nicaragua War."

[14] Jessie Katz, Claire Spiegel, and Ralph Frammolino, "Probe Finds No Crack Conspiracy," *The Seattle Times – Today's Top Stories, National News*, [http://www.seattletimes.com/extra/browse/html/altcrac_102096.html], 20October 1996.

[15] Ibid.

[16] Ibid.

was unsure about "whether [Freeway Ricky] Ross' Nicaraguan ring was the first to bring cocaine to Los Angeles' African-American neighborhoods." Nevertheless, he did believe that Ross, through his Nicaraguan connections, was the first to import cocaine in large amounts that the south-central Los Angeles residents could afford.[17]

John Deutch, CIA Director at the time of the *San Jose Mercury News* allegations indicating CIA involvement in drug trafficking, asked the agency's Inspector General to investigate the charges. On January 29, 1998, the CIA released a "Report of Investigations." After an extensive examination of documents, and numerous interviews with relevant persons across the United States and on four continents by a 17-person team working with the Department of Justice, Office of the Inspector General, the report stated, "No information was found to indicate that any past or present employee of CIA, or anyone acting on behalf of CIA, had any direct or indirect dealing with Ricky Ross, Oscar Danillo Blandon or Juan Norwin Meneses" (another major drug trafficker allegedly connected with the contras and the CIA).[18]

A final explanation about the transition from cocaine freebase abuse to crack cocaine is associated with the decline of the drug paraphernalia industry between 1982 and 1984. The decline resulted in a shortage of cocaine smoking accessories, which led to the common use of the baking soda processing method and eliminated the need for special chemicals and glassware.[19] Crack use brought about a change in the strategy for selling and marketing smokable cocaine. Prior to crack's appearance, cocaine freebase users prepared their own product for large amounts of cocaine hydrochloride. Crack, however, was preprocessed and ready-made for consumers in single doses that could be smoked immediately. Furthermore, since it was provided in small vials that contained one or two rocks, user had to purchase the drug more frequently to maintain their daily dose regimens.[20]

A common thread appears in five of the six accounts. The price of cocaine could be reduced when it was sold in the form of crack, and could be purchased in some areas for as little as $2.00 per vial, and users could even

---

[17] Ibid.

[18] Central Intelligence Agency, Inspector General, *Report of Investigation: Allegations of Connections Between CIA and the Contras in Cocaine Trafficking to the United States, Vol. 1: The California Story*, 96-0143-IG (29 January 1998), 6. The CIA reported that over 365 interviews were conducted, mostly under oath, with current and former CIA employees, other current and former federal government officials, private citizens, and foreign nationals.

[19] Siegel, "Repeating Cycles of Cocaine Use and Abuse," 299.

[20] Ibid., 103.

obtain a puff from a crack pipe for 75 cents.[21] In the form of crack, cocaine was no longer the drug for the wealthy but became affordable for virtually anyone, even the unemployed or a teenage drug user.[22] The conclusion of the matter, however, is that crack use quickly rose in popularity, and its uses spread across the nation in a very short period of time. How crack use and abuse spread so rapidly is explored in the following section.

---

[21] Department of Justice, Drug Enforcement Administration, *Crack Cocaine: Drug Intelligence Report* (April 1994), 4.

[22] Ibid., 2.

Chapter 5

HOW CRACK COCAINE
ABUSE SPREAD NATIONWIDE

South America is the primary source of cocaine for the United States.[1] In the 1980's, the main cocaine distribution areas in the United States were Los Angeles, Miami, and New York.[2] Consequently, those cities were the first to be inundated with crack and were the principal source cities for the nation's crack supply.[3]

The DEA reported that crack was first available in Los Angeles and Miami in 1981 (it was found in Houston as well),[4] and in New York as early as 1983.[5] Drug use/abuse researcher and writer, James A. Inciardi of the University of Delaware, appeared to corroborate those findings in his book, *The War on Drugs II: the Continuing Epic of Heroin, Cocaine, Crack, Crime, AIDS, and Public Policy,* when he surmised that the "rediscovery" of crack or "baking soda freebase" occurred simultaneously on both the west

---

[1] House Committee on the Judiciary, Subcommittee on Crime, *Drug Production and Trafficking in Latin America and the Caribbean: Hearings,* 98ᵗʰ Cong., 1ˢᵗ Sess., 12 May 1983, 4.

[2] Drug Enforcement administration, *Crack Cocaine: Drug Intelligence Report,* 4.

[3] Massing, "Crack's Destructive Sprint Across America," 58.

[4] A contradiction was found in DEA data concerning the year that crack was first available in Miami. Three DEA reports stated that in 1981, crack was available in Los Angeles, San Diego, and Houston *(The Crack Situation in the United States,* September 1986, 4: *Crack Cocaine Availability and Trafficking in the United States,* January 1988,1; and *Crack Cocaine: Overview 1989,* 1) The september 1986 report specifically stated that "crack was first noted in 1984" in Miami. Another DEA Report, *Crack Cocaine: Drug Intelligence Report,* April, 1994, included Miami in its list of cities where crack was first available in 1981. CRS used the 1981 date because it was included in the later DEA report for which more accurate information might have been acquired, and because other sources, mentioned in the body of this report, placed crack in Miami by 1982.

[5] Drug Enforcement Administration, *Crack Cocaine: Drug Intelligence Report,* 39.

and east coasts in the early 1980's.[6] His account is similar to that of Michael aldrich who reported (see p. 15-16) that crack cocaine arrived in Miami via Caribbean chemists. At the same time in Los Angeles, Inciardi stated, a basement chemist was rediscovering the baking soda method of preparing freebase.[7]

Gordon Witkin, in his article, "the Men Who Created Crack," when discussing how rock arrived in Los Angeles and Miami, provided a very similar time frame, but specifically state that rock appeared in Los Angeles in 1980. Furthermore, he related that a 1982 Miami Police Department raid on five drug houses run by a Caribbean immigrant in two poor neighborhoods was a major signal that crack had arrived in Miami. One of the officers involved in the raid revealed that this was the first time he had seen "rocks." A Caribbean immigrant claimed to have invented the substance. Therefore, that evidence suggests that crack had arrived in Miami by 1982. Witkin went on to say that authorities believed that there was probably a race between Californian and Caribbean distributors to see who could introduce crack to the New York City market first.[8]

In December 1983, a former Bronx, New York narcotics policeman who directed a "street research unit" reported hearing two drug abusers in the Tremont section of the Bronx talk about a new drug called crack and/or rock cocaine being used in the area. It was nearly one year later, in 1984, before that officer saw an individual who actually was smoking the drug. He learned at the time that this form of cocaine freebase was made with baking soda instead of ether. By the end of 1985, he stated, the drug had saturated the city.[9]

The DEA reported that Jamaican gangs, called "posses," operating out of New York city, and the Los Angeles-based street gangs known as "the Crips" and "the Bloods" were the most proficient nationwide crack distributors that resided in the three principal source cities. Other major selling organizations were groups of Haitians and Dominicans.[10] Expanding from the three source cities, these groups used similar distribution techniques that involved interstate and intrastate transporting of wholesale amounts of crack and cocaine. These organizations appeared to be dividing the country between them, one source observed, with the Los Angeles gangs working eastward from California and the Jamaican posses working westward from

[6] Inciardi, *The War on Drugs II,* 111.

[7] Ibid., 112.

[8] Witkin et al, "The Men Who Created Crack," 49.

[9] Ibid.

[10] Drug Enforcement Administration, *Crack Cocaine: Drug Intelligence Report,* 4.

New York.[11] The DEA stated that the nationwide spread of crack also was fueled by the involvement of local street gangs in various cities. In addition, other groups such as Cubans, Guyanese, and Colombians, became active in interstate transport and distribution of crack after its initial arrival in the early 1980's.[12]

Whether crack cocaine initially was spread by organized gangs is a subject of debate. In a 1994 article, James C. Howell reported that over the past decade (i.e. during the 1980s) not much empirical research documented that drug trafficking networks were organized and operated by youth gangs. In some cases, however, older former gang members of the Crips and Bloods and "wannabes" who were supplied by the Los Angeles gangs, organized and operated the networks.[13] Furthermore, he cited a 1985 Los Angeles study that indicated that drug trafficking was not a primary gang activity, but many individual gang members were involved in distributing drugs. The year of the study, 1985, however, was the year prior to the influx of crack cocaine in the nation, and drug trafficking probably was not a priority for the Crips and Bloods at that time. Howell mentions several other research studies (one as early as 1984, but others from 1988 and 1989, when crack abuse was very prominent) that do attribute high levels of drug dealing to gang members. On the other hand, a 1993 study he cited also contended that crack distribution was neither gang controlled nor an organized activity.[14] Therefore, the true involvement of gangs in the distribution of crack cocaine is not clear.

Table 1 lists the cities that some sources believe were infiltrated by the Crips and Bloods. **Table 2** lists the cities some sources believe were infiltrated by the Jamaican posses.

By 1989, the DEA reported that crack cocaine, which primarily was an urban drug abuse problem confined to minority neighborhoods,[15] had been distributed from the large source cities (which later included Detroit), to smaller cities, towns, suburbs, and rural areas in virtually every state across the nation, including Alaska and Hawaii.[16] **Table 3** lists the cities where crack appeared between 1981 and early 1986, and provides the year it was first noted, the organization reportedly supplying the drug to the area, and reported local crack distributors.

---

[11] Massing, "Crack's Destructive Sprint Across America," 58.

[12] Drug Enforcement Administration, *Crack Cocaine: Drug Intelligence Report,* 32, 35, 38.

[13] James C. Howell, "Recent Gang Research: Program and Policy Implications," *Crime & Delinquency,* 40 (October 1994), 507.

[14] Ibid., 508.

[15] Drug Enforcement Administration, *Crack Cocaine: Overview 1989,* 13.

[16] Drug Enforcement administration, *Crack Cocaine: Drug Intelligence Report,* 16; and Ibid.

**Table 1. Nationwide Crack Distribution by
Los Angeles-Based Street Gangs Crips and Bloods**

From Los Angeles North To:	1. Sacramento 2. Reno 3. Portland 4. Seattle
From Los Angeles, Northeast To:	5. Las Vegas 6. Salt Lake City 7. Denver 8. Minneapolis 9. Omaha 10. York, PA 11. Baltimore
From Los Angeles, East To:	12. Phoenix 13. Tucson 14. Shreveport 15. Oklahoma city 16. St. Louis 17. Kansas City

Table 2. Nationwide Crack Infiltration by the Jamaican Posses

From Jamaica to Miami, North To:	1. Atlanta 2. Charlotte 3. Wilmington, N.C. 4. Roanoke 5. Norfolk
From Jamaica to New York City, South To:	6. Philadelphia 7. Baltimore 8. Washington D.C. 9. Martinsburg, VA
From New York City, North To:	10. Hartford 11. Boston
From New York City, Northwest To:	12. Toronto, Canada 13. Rochester 14. Buffalo 15. Minneapolis
From New York City, West To:	16. Cleveland 17. Columbus 18. Kansas City, MO 19. Denver 20. Houston 21. Los Angeles

Source: Tables 1 and 2 were compiled by the Congressional Research service (CRS) from information contained in an article by Gordon Witkin et al., "The Men Who Created Crack," *U.S. News and World Report*, 19 August 1991, 46.

Table 3. Initial Crack Cocaine Availability
(By City, Year, Group and Local Distributors)

City	Year Noted	Group Distributor	Local Primary Distributor
Atlanta	Early 1986	Miami-connected organized street gangs	Migrant farm worker from Florida.[a]
Boston	August 1985	Couriers from New York City, Philadelphia, West Coast, Canada	African Americans and Dominicans
Chicago	Late 1985/Early 1986[b]	None[c]	African American Street gangs and freelance sellers
Dallas	Early 1986	LA street gangs[d] and Jamaican posses	Could be found in low-income African American and Hispanic areas.
Denver	Late 1985	LA street gangs and Jamaican posses	African American and Hispanic street gangs
Detroit	Early 1986	Colombians and Cubans	African American organizations or street gangs
Houston	1981	Black Colombians	African American street gangs
Kansas City, MO	In 1986 crack was readily and increasingly available.	Jamaican posses	Not specified
Los Angeles	1981	LA street gangs	LA street gangs

City	Year Noted	Group Distributor	Local Primary Distributor
Miami	1981[e]	Primarily Jamaicans, Haitians, and African Americans[f]	African Americans
Minneapolis	Late 1985	None	Not Specified
Newark	Late 1985	Transported from New York City	Not specified
New Orleans	Not specified	LA street gangs and Jamaican posses	African American street gangs
New York City	Possibly 1983. Officially noted in late 1985	Dominicans, Jamaican posses, African American gangs	Independent operators, Dominican gangs, Jamaican posses, African American gangs
Philadelphia	Not specified	Certain ethnic groups African Americans, Jamaicans, Puerto Ricans, and other Hispanics	Many ethnic groups
Phoenix	Early 1986	LA street gangs and Jamaican posses	Not specified
San Diego	1981	LA street gangs and Jamaican posses	African Americans supplied by local and Mexican and Cuban groups
San Francisco	Not specified	LA street gangs	African Americans
Seattle	1985[g]	LA street gangs and Mexican traffickers	African Americans connected to organized street gangs
St. Louis	Mid-1985	LA street gangs	African American street gangs

City	Year Noted	Group Distributor	Local Primary Distributor
Washington, D.C.	Early 1986	Miami and New York city groups, particularly Jamaican posses	African American street gangs, called "crews"

Source: Compiled by CRS using information presented in two DEA reports — *The Crack Cocaine Situation in the United States,* September 1986, and *Crack Caocaine: Drug Intelligence Report,* April 1994.

[a] In contrast to other parts of the country, crack was introduced to African American rural communities in the Atlanta area by migrant farm workers from Florida.

[b] Although crack was available in Chicago urban areas, the drug was not widely available or abused there until late 1990 and early 1991.

[c] The DEA reported that Los Angeles-based street gangs (Bloods and Crips) were successfully prohibited from creating crack distribution organizations or crack hoses in Chicago by the efforts of local police and local street gangs.

[d] LA street gangs refer to Los Angeles-based Bloods and Crips.

[e] There was ambiguity in DEA information concerning the year crack first was noted in Miami. The September 1986 DEA report indicated that crack was first noted there in 1984. The April 1994 DEA study state 1981 as the year of its arrival. CRS chose to use 1981 because of other sources that placed the drug in Miami by 1982.

[f] Other groups were reportedly becoming established as well, i.e., Guyanese and Nicaraguans. Also, Bahamians were importing crack into Miami via cruise ships.

[g] the September 1986 DEA report indicated 1985, while the April 1994 report stated 1986. CRS is using 1985 because that was the date used in the later 1994 report, for which more accurate information might have been acquired.

Chapter 6

THE EXTENT OF NATIONWIDE
CRACK COCAINE ABUSE

Because of crack's spread nationwide in a short period of time, crack abuse was considered by many observers to have reached epidemic proportions by the end of 1986 or 1987. Some commentators, however, questioned whether there actually was a nationwide crack epidemic, or whether it only was portrayed as such in the media. Drug abuse researcher James Inciardi stated in his book, *The War on Drugs II,* that the front page story in the November 29, 1985 *New York Times* entitled, "A New Purified Form of Cocaine Causes Alarm As Abuse Increases," started the concentrated media coverage of crack use and abuse.[1] Other newspapers, such as the *Washington Post* and the *Los Angeles Times,* as well as news magazines, such as *Newsweek, Time,* and *U.S. News and World Report,* published over 1,000 stories among them prominently focusing on crack. During this period, CBS television presented a special news program entitled, "48 Hours on Crack Street," while NBC broadcast "Cocaine Country," a news special at the end of a six-month period in which over 400 reports had been televised about drug abuse.[2]

"Crack Hysteria" mounted during the summer of 1986, Inciardi stated, as *Newsweek* reported that crack was the biggest story since Vietnam and the fall of the Nixon presidency. Other media sources compared the spread of crack with the plagues in medieval Europe.[3] University of Texas researchers, however, examined the extent to which the media might have influenced

---

[1] Inciardi, *The War on Drugs II,* 106.
[2] Ibid.
[3] Ibid., 106-107.

each other, which the analysts referred to as "intermedia agenda setting."[4] They suggested that the cocaine issue of 1985 and 1986 had more to do with intermedia agenda setting than with the structure of society, real-world indicators, or sensational news events, although all of those factors played some role in many stories. Their conclusions were based on the belief that actual cocaine use and abuse had risen. Also, they felt that although the "new drug" crack, was a problem in certain urban areas, there was no evidence of a "real drug epidemic."[5]

In agreement with this assessment, drug abuse researchers, Inciardi reported, were not finding crack to be a national epidemic, as was being portrayed by the media, but an isolated phenomenon in a few inner-city communities that were in fewer than 12 urban areas.[6] Similarly, the DEA, in its September 1986 Special Report: *The Crack Situation in the United States,* indicated that crack was available in 13 cities; it found some level of a availability in four additional cities and Washington, D.C., for a total of 18 urban areas.[7] In its 1994 report, the DEA indicated that between 1981 and early 1986, crack cocaine was available in 20 cities and Washington, D.C., for a total of 21 urban areas (see **Table 3,** pp. 23-25). Those data did not suggest that crack use was an isolated phenomenon, but whether they indicated a national drug epidemic is debatable. Furthermore, in its 1986 report, the DEA noted what appeared to be undue attention to the problem by observing,

> Crack is currently the subject of considerable media attention. The result has been a distortion of the public perception of the extent of crack use as compared to the use of other drugs. With multi-kilogram quantities of cocaine hydrochloride available and with snorting continuing to be the primary route of cocaine administration, crack presently appears to be a secondary rather than a primary problem in most areas. Additionally, a number of drug treatment and prevention specialists fear that this flood of media coverage and the occasional glamorous depiction of drug use by the entertainment industry could combine to act as a catalyst for some abusers seeking a more euphoric effect.[8]

---

[4] Lucig H. Danielian, and Stephen D. Reese, "A Closer look at Intermedia Influences on Agenda Setting: Th Cocaine Issue of 1986," in *Communication Campaigns About Drugs,* 47-66.

[5] Ibid., 47.

[6] Inciardi, The War on Drugs II, 107.

[7] Drug Enforcement Administration, *The Crack Situation in the United States,* 4.

[8] Ibid., 2.

Inciardi concluded from his observations that the drug abuse professionals, who were skeptical about the news reports on the permeation of society by crack, and the media were both correct in their perceptions, but wrong at the same time. He believed that, contrary to media portrayals, during the summer and fall of 1986, crack was not yet an epidemic, but began to become a prominent problem in early 1987.[9] At the July 1986 Joint hearing of the House Select Committee on Narcotica Abuse and Control and Select Committee on Children, Youth, and Families assessing the crack cocaine issue, a DEA official stated that crack had emerged as a major drug problem in less than one year.[10] On the other hand, another investigator observed that "it is not at all clear whether crack use had increased during early 1986, the extent to which crack was responsible for health and behavioral problems, or crack's actual effects on crime. However, the drug certainly began drawing the attention of the media, and crack seemed to satisfy the feeding frenzy of the anti-drug crusaders."[11]

EPIDEMIC DEFINED AND EXAMINED

To determine whether there was a national crack cocaine epidemic, the term is defined and data considered to see whether they meet the criteria of the definition. The Centers for Disease Control and Prevention (CDC), an agency within the Public Health Service of the Department of Health and Human Services, with the mission "to promote health and quality of life by preventing and controlling disease, injury, and disability,"[12] provides the following definition of an epidemic:

> The occurrence in a community or region of cases on an illness, specific health-related behavior, or other health-related events clearly in excess of normal expectancy. The community or region and the period in which the cases occur are specified precisely. The number of cases indicating the presence of an epidemic varies according to the agent, size, and type of population exposed, previous experience or lack of exposure to the disease, and time and place of occurrence, epidemicity is thus relative to usual

---

[9] Inciardi, *The War on Drugs II*, 108.

[10] House Select Committee on Narcortics abuse and Control, and the Select Committee on Children, Youth, and Families, *The Crack Cocaine Crisis: Joint Hearing*, 99th Cong., 2nd Sess., 15 July 1986, 148.

[11] Steven R. Belenko, *Crack and the Evolution of Anti-Drug Policy*, 6.

[12] The Centers for Disease Control and Prevention, "About CDC," [http://www.cdc.gov/aboutcdc.htm#mission]. No date.

frequency of the disease in the same area, among the specified population, at the same season of the year.[13]

An epidemic, according to the definition, occurs when health-related events are "clearly in excess of normal expectancy." The "normal expectancy" for drug abuse in a population, according to one drug abuse expert, however, has not been established. Furthermore, when using the criteria in the CDC's definition of epidemic, it cannot be accurately determined that one occurred nationally for crack cocaine abuse, because there is no way to get accurate data to make that decision.[14] Therefore, on the basis of the CDC definition it is not clear that there was a nationwide crack cocaine epidemic in 1986-87, or at any time.

On the other hand, another expert observed that although there is no clearly determined "normal expectancy" for drug abuse, if available data that recorded drug use in the nation before crack cocaine abuse became a problem could be compared with distinctive increases shown by the data at the time when crack was reported as a problem, it could be determined whether those changes were clearly in excess of the originally noted drug useage. If the data showed crack use clearly exceeding previous levels of drug use, they could indicate an epidemic.[15]

In June 1986, it was reported that no data were available from the DEA or NIDA indicating how many people in the nation had tried crack.[16] Consequently, no accurate prevalence or incidence[17] data were located for the 1986-1987 period that could be used to determine the nationwide extent of crack abuse. There were some prevalence and incidence data collected indicating that crack cocaine abuse probably caused serious problems among older youth and adults ages 18 years and above, during the 1986-87 time period. Such resources are discussed below.

---

[13] *A Dictionary of Epidemiology,* 3rd ed., ed. John M. Last and J.H. Abramson, et al. (New York: Oxford University Press, 1995), 54.

[14] James A. Iciardi, telephone conversation with author, 20 May 1998.

[15] Eric Wish, telephone conversation with author, 20 May 1998.

[16] David Holtzman, "Hot Line Taking 1,200 Calls A Day," *Insight,* 23 June 1986, 48.

[17] Prevalence and incidence rates are the two primary ways to measure the extent of an illness or in this instance, the emergence and spread of a specific health-related behavior. Prevalence rates refer to the actual number of individuals who have an illness at a particular time, while incidence rates pertain to the number of new cases that occur during a certain period of time – Daniel m. Wilner, Rosabelle P. Walkley, and Edward J. O'Neill, *Introduction to Public Health,* 7th ed., (New York: Macmillan Publishing co., 1978), 331-332.
The most popular epidemiological measure of drug use, however, is the prevalence ratio (counts/frequencies) – Thomas M. Mieczkowski, "The Prevalence of Drug Use in the United States," *Crime and Justice* 20 (1996): 354.

Indicators from Available Data Sources

Three NIDA-supported projects provided some clues about the initial impact of crack cocaine use and abuse upon the nation. They were the National Household Survey on Drug Abuse (NHSDA)[18] "Monitoring the future: A continuing study of the Lifestyles and Values of Youth," also known as the "National High School Senior Survey" (NHSSS), and the Drug Abuse Warning Network (DAWN). In addition to these projects was a drug abuse measuring program called the Drug Use Forecasting (DUF) program sponsored by the Department of Justice's National Institute of Justice (NIJ). Some of the strengths and limitations of theses resources, related to data collection and the groups surveyed, are discussed below.

The National Household Survey on Drug Abuse

The NHSDA has been sponsored by NIDA since the Institute's creation in 1974. The survey provides information on the use of illicit drugs, alcohol and tobacco among U.S. household members who are 12 years old and above. The number of individuals who use those drugs are recorded to reflect various demographic characteristics, such as age, sex, race, residential region, and others. Also noted are frequency and pattern of use, problems resulting from use, and the person's perception of risks involved in using the products.[19] The survey is taken through interviews of household populations that are representative of the continental United States (Alaska and Hawaii are omitted). A completed survey must contain, at a minimum, data on the lifetime use of illicit drugs, alcohol, and tobacco. Also, responders are asked about use of those products within the past year and past month.[20]

Since 1974, the survey has been conducted every two to three years, except in 1976 and 1977 when it was done consecutively. Subsequently, surveys were taken in 1985 and 1988, thereby missing 1986 and 1987, the crucial primary years of crack cocaine abuse. For the 1988 report, however, 87% of the interviews were conducted by December31, 1988.[21] The NHSDA did not include questions specifically related to crack cocaine use until 1988.

---

[18] The National Household Survey on drug Abuse and the Drug abuse Warning Network are sponsored by the Substance Abuse and Mental Health Services Administration (SAMHSA), which was created in 1992.

[19] Department of Health and Human Services, Public Health Service, Alcohol, drug abuse, and Mental Health Administration, National Institute on Drug Abuse, *National Household Survey on Drug Abuse: Main Findings 1988*, (1990), 1.

[20] Ibid., 7.

[21] Department of Health and Human Services, *National Household Survey on Drug Abuse: Main Findings 1988* , 4-5.

Therefore, responses regarding use of cocaine within the last year, for the 1988 report, could represent such drug use in 1987.

NHSDA results indicated that for 1988 there was very small percentage of crack users. Of all household members aged 12 years and older, 1.3% had used crack one or more times during their lifetimes,[22] 0.5% had used it in the past year, and 1.1% used it within the past month.[23] Responses related to population, density and regional use showed that crack was more commonly used by residents in large metropolitan areas and among persons living in the northeastern and western areas of the country. (See **Table 4**).

Although these data indicated that the rates of crack use were low, the NHSDA report stated that in 1988 there were about half a million persons in the nation's household population who had used the drug in the month before the interview. Also, 2.5 million people in the household population had used crack one or more times in their lives.[24]

A 1993 General Accounting Office (GAO) report discussing drug use measurement concluded that NHSDA national drug prevalence rates should be considered as "conservative approximations." Although the NHSDA is the only national estimate of household cocaine prevalence rates available, it stated, the study has traditionally excluded several groups of people who are at high risk for drug use but who so not live in households.[25] NIDA revealed that the survey does not include the homeless, incarcerated, institutionalized, military personnel, college dormitory students, or people living in group homes.[26] In addition, surveyors rely on the truthfulness of the participants, and a 20% to 30% range of nonresponse often occurs, varying among age, sex, and race subgroups.[27] Since NHSDA used the data to project the drug use patterns of the total U.S. population, inaccurate estimates might exist.

---

[22] Ibid., 58.

[23] Ibid., 57.

[24] Department of Health and Human Services, Public Health Service, Alcohol, Drug Abuse, and Mental Health Administration, National Institute on Drug Abuse, *National Household Survey on Drug Abuse: Highlights 1988,* (1990), 28.

[25] General Accounting Office, *Drug Use Measurement: Strengths, Limitations, and Recommendations for Improvement,* GAO/PEMD-93-18, June 1993, 56.

[26] Department of Health and Human Services, *National Household Survey on Drug Abuse: Main Findings 1988*, 4.

[27] Jeff Lean, "Number Jumble Clouds Judgement of Drug War: Differing Surveys, Analyses Yield Unreliable Data," *The Washington Post*, Friday, 2 January 1998, A20.

**Table 4. National Household Survey on Drug Abuse,
1988 Percentage Reporting Crack Use in the Past Year,
by Age-Group and Demographic Variable**

Demographic variable	12-to-17 Years	18-to-25 Years	26-to-34 Years	Over 35 Years
SEX				
Male	0.5	2.0	0.8	*
Female	0.8	1.8	0.6	*
RACE				
White	0.7	1.7	0.4	*
Black	*	*	2.3	*
Hispanic	0.9	3.5	1.3	*
POPULATION DENSITY	1.0	2.2	1.1	*
Large Metro	*	1.9	*	*
Small Metro	*	*	*	*
Nonmetro				
REGION				
Northeast	*	3.6	0.9	*
North central	1.4	*	*	*
South	*	1.4	0.6	*
West	*	3.0	1.1	*

Source: Compiled by CRS from, information in Table 4.9 of the National Household survey on drug abuse, Main findings 1988, p. 59.
*Low precision; no estimate reported.

Furthermore, the GAO found that the 1988 NHSDA data did not reflect a large nonresponse rate pattern of cocaine users that occurred in geographic areas in which at least 10% of the population used drugs.[28] The 1988 NHSDA study data did not indicate an extensive nationwide crack cocaine problem during 1987. As the GAO study concluded, however, results probably reflected a significant underreporting, because there were so many groups excluded from the survey. Many members of these non-household populations might have been high risk for crack use, and if included, might have revealed a larger percentage of crack usage among the total U.S. population.

---

[28] General accounting Office, *Drug Use Measurement*, 56.

National High School Senior Survey

In 1975, "The Monitoring the Future: a Continuing Study of the Lifestyles and Values of Youth," also known as the "National High School Senior Survey" (NHSSS)[29] , was originated at the University of Michigan through its Institute for Social Research. Sponsored by NIDA grants, illicit drug use by U.S. high school seniors is annually recorded and analyzed, as well as student attitudes noted toward drug use. Each year about 16,000 to 17,000 high school seniors are canvassed through a written questionnaire in about 135 or so (ranging between 120 and 140) high schools across the nation. The sample is chosen to be representative of all seniors in the continental United States. Students are asked if they used illicit drugs at least once during their lifetime, within the previous year (termed annual use), and/or within the last 30 days (termed current use).[30]

The NHSS reported that questions about crack cocaine use were included in the survey in 1986. Participants were asked whether they had used cocaine within the last 12 months, and if crack was one of the drug forms used. Before 1986, indicators collected by the survey provided some indirect evidence of the swift spread of crack. For example, it reported that the rate of all seniors indicating they smoked cocaine freebase more than doubled between 1983 and 1986, rising from 2.4% to 5.7%. Furthermore, there were some signs of compulsive use or craving for the smoked drug in those who reported using cocaine the year prior to the survey. The percentage doubled from 0.4% to 0.8% of seniors who reported that they could not stop using the smokable cocaine when they tried. In addition, between 1984 and 1986, the number of seniors who reported an active daily use of the drug doubled, rising from 0.2% to 0.4%. Surveyors believed that the arrival of crack cocaine during that period of time contributed to those increases.[31]

In 1987, questions about crack cocaine use were included in two questionnaire forms. Subsequent results from the poll disclosed that between 1986 and 1991, crack use declined among high school seniors by about 60%, falling from 4.1% to 1.5%.[32] Furthermore, in 1987 the rate of seniors who

---

[29] Other sources have used different acronyms for this survey such as, MTF for Monitoring the Future, and HSSS for High School Senior Survey.

[30] The University of Michigan, News and Information Services, *News Release,* 28 February 1989, 1-2.

[31] Department of Health and Human Services, National Institute on Drug Abuse, *National Survey Results on Drug Use from the Monitoring The Future Study, 1975-1995: Volume 1, Secondary School Students,* by Lloyd D. Johnston, Patrick M. O'Malley, and Jerald G. Bachman, the University of Michigan, Institute for Social research (1996), 95.

[32] Ibid., 105.

used crack within their lifetime was first measured and found to be 5.4%.[33] By 1992, this rate had declined by one-half to 2.6%. Figures for current crack use or within the last 30-days indicated a decline from 1.3% to 0.7% in 1990.[34] Those declines indicated that crack abuse did not appear to be a major problem among high school seniors between 1986 and 1992, although there were increases in cocaine and/or crack use between 1983 and 1986.

The GAO study concluded that, although considered to be the best early warning system for drug use among teens. NHSSS results, similar to the NHSDA findings, should be considered as conservative estimates of the national prevalence rate of drug use among high school seniors. The NHSSS relies on the truthfulness of those surveyed, omits school dropouts and absentees, and does not adequately measure nonwhite drug users.[35]

Because of underreporting of data due to excluding certain high risk groups and inadequately measuring others, NHSSS data do not appear to accurately reflect the crack cocaine situation during the time of its initial prominence in 1986-87. According to the NHSSS surveyors, crack use and/or abuse, relative to other illicit drugs, occurred more among what they termed the "out-of-school population," i.e., persons 18 years and older.[36]

There were no NHSSS data that reflected crack use among the "out-of-school" population, since drug use among this group is not measured. Data collected by the Drug Abuse Warning Network (discussed below), which reported the numbers of individuals suffering from smokable cocaine-related medical emergency episodes, do indicate that a larger number of persons 18 years and older suffered such emergencies than did those within the younger age groups. Those data, however, did not accurately reflect that more people 18 years and older actually used the drug (see **Table 6** and the discussion below).

---

[33] A University of Michigan news release dated February 28, 1989 reported a slightly different rate of 5.6%.

[34] Department of Health and Human Services, *National Survey Results on Drug Use*, 105.

[35] General accounting Office, *Drug Use Measurement*, 57.

[36] Leen, "Number Jumble," *The Washington Post*, A20.

Table 5. National High School Senior Survey, Percentage Reporting Either Smokable Cocaine, Cocaine, or Crack Use, 1983-1992

Year* of Survey Results	Smoked Cocaine in Past Year	Felt Compulsion to Use Smokable Cocaine in Past Year	Daily Cocaine Use	Current Crack Use	Used Crack in Past Year	Lifetime Crack Use
1983	2.4	0.4	-----	-----	-----	-----
1984	-----	-----	0.2	-----	-----	-----
1986	5.7	0.8	0.4	-----	4.1	-----
1987	-----	-----	-----	1.3	4.0	5.4
1988	-----	-----	-----	-----	3.1	4.8
1990	-----	-----	-----	0.7	-----	-----
1991	-----	-----	-----	-----	1.5	-----
1992	-----	-----	-----	-----	-----	2.6

Source: Compiled by CRS from data reported in the report, National Survey results on Drug Use From the Monitoring the Future Study, 1975-1995; Volume 1, Secondary School Students (see footnote 152).

*Data were available only for the years indicated.

Drug Abuse Warning Network

In the early 1970's, the DEA implemented DAWN to collect data from persons seeking hospital emergency room assistance that was related to illegal drug use or the nonmedical use of a legal drug. Thos data included person who overdosed on illicit drugs, as well as those who attempted suicide by taking legal drugs. The data were used for several purposes – "to identify substances associated with emergency room episodes, to assess health consequences associated with drug abuse, and to monitor trends and patterns in drug abuse."[1] Data were obtained from over 500 emergency hospital rooms in 21 cities.[2]

DAWN data revealed that cocaine-related hospital emergencies were concentrated in individuals 18 years and older. **Table 6** shows DAWN data depicting this situation from 1985 to 1988. Sharp increased in the numbers of such emergencies can be observed for individuals 18 and up. Particularly striking are the increases in such episodes from 1985 to 1986. For persons 18 to 25 years old, an 85% rise in episodes occurred, while a 78% increase took place among 26 to 34-year olds, and a 69% increase was recorded among persons 35 and older. From 1986 to 1987, however, the 35-and-older age group is the only one that incurred a large increase, 98%, in cocaine-related emergencies.

Table 6. Cocaine-Related Hospital Emergency Department Episode Estimates by Age of User, 1985-1988

	Year			
Age	**1985**	**1986**	**1987**	**1988**
12-to-17- Years	1,006	1,803	2,538	2,755
18-to25	9,386	17,362	29,382	32,322
26-to34	12,904	22,987	41,039	44,632
35+	5,494	9,317	18,489	21,634
Total U.S.	28,827	51,666	91,791	101,578

Source: Compiled by CRS from data in the U.S. Department of Health and Human Service's Substance Abuse and Mental Health Services Administration (SAMSHA) Advance Report Number 16, *Historical Estimates From the Drug Abuse Warning Network*, p. 40.

---

[1] Jonathan P. Caulkins et al., "Describing DAWN's Dominion," *Contemporary Drug Problems*, 22 (Fall 1995): 547.

[2] Department of Health and Human Services, Public Health Service, Substance Abuse and Mental Health Services Administration, Office of applied Studies, *Historical Estimates From the Drug Abuse Warning Network: 1987-94 Estimates of Drug-Related Emergency Department Episodes*, Advance Report number 16, (August 1996), 40.

In 1984 and 1985, hospital emergency cocaine-related admissions for problems involving smoking as the primary route of administration were relatively few compared with those for the more traditional routes – injection and sniffing/snorting. In 1986, however, there was a large increase in cocaine smoking cases.[3] **Table 7** shows slightly less than a four-fold growth in cocaine smoking-related emergency room episodes from 1985 to 1986. Furthermore, from 1986 to 1987, such incidents increased again nearly three-fold. In 1987, however, cocaine smoke-related emergency episodes were slightly outnumbered by the injection-related cases. In 1988, smoke-related cased began to dominate such admissions, with a 17% growth, while cocaine injections decreased by 5%. These striking changes have been attributed to the widespread abuse of crack cocaine beginning in the mid-1980s.[4] At the same time, however, cocaine-related emergency cases with other or unknown routes of administration alarmingly increased more than five-fold from 1985 to 1988.

Table 7. Cocaine–Related Hospital Emergency Department Episode Estimates, By Route of Administration 1985-1988

Route of Administration	1985	1986	1987	1988
Smoke	2,264	8,717	23,535	27,629
Injection	10,854	15,001	23,548	22,347
Sniff/Snort	9,238	13,085	15,174	14,119
Other/Unknown	6,470	14,864	29,535	37,482
Total U.S.	28,827	51,666	91,791	101,578

Source: Compiled by CRS from data in the U.S. Department of Health and Human Service's Substance Abuse and Mental Health services Administration (SAMSHA) advance Report Number 16, *Historical Estimates From the Drug Abuse Warning Network,* p.40.

DAWN has been called the "best measure of people with chronic or acute drug problems" because it collected data from patients visiting emergency rooms in over 500 hospitals in 21 cities.[5] Between 1986 and 1988 when crack abuse was initially prominent, however, DAWN's data collection was limited because it was not based on a representative sample of nationwide hospital emergency rooms. In 1980, NIDA assumed

---

[3] Ibid.

[4] Ibid., 13.

[5] Leen, "Number Jumble," *The Washington Post,*A20.

responsibility for DAWN and reported that after 1988, data were based on a representative sample of nonfederal, "short-stay" hospitals with 24-hour emergency departments.[6] DAWN did not record drug-related emergencies in any Veterans Administration hospitals or in any similar federal hospital facilities. Furthermore, it did not count drug-related episodes in places other than hospital emergency rooms.[7]

In spite of those weaknesses, DAWN statistics suggested substantial increases in cocaine abusers between 1985 and 1988 by indicating significant increases in cocaine-related emergencies. According to a drug abuse researcher analyzing the DAWN system, however, the chief problem with using DAWN data to determine the extent of drug abuse in society is that "only a small and not necessarily representative fraction of drug users demand emergency treatment. Thus, the absolute numbers of DAWN mentions need bear little relation to the number of users"[8] therefore, since a small number of drug abusers actually report to hospital emergency rooms for treatment, DAWN data underreport actual cocaine and particularly smokable cocaine abusers. This implies, similarly to NHSD and NHSSS results, that the national problem might have been much worse than could be determined via the DAWN data collections.

Drug Use Forecasting Program

In early 1987, the National Institute of Justice, the primary research agency of the Department of Justice, created the Drug Use Forecasting (DUF)[9] program. DUF is the only drug use measurement tool that assesses a high risk population. The purpose of the program was to provide local level estimates of recent drug use by persons arrested in the largest cities in the nation. Trained local staff in 24 cities across the nation monitor arrestee volunteers at central booking facilities within 48 hours after arrest to obtain drug use information through urine tests and personal interviews.[10] Interviewers first select participants who are charged with nondrug offences. The aim is to have a representative sample of persons charged with a variety

---

[6] Department of Health and Human Services, *Historical Estimates From the Drug Abuse Warning Network: 1978-94*, 40.

[7] Caulkins et al., "Describing DAWN's Dominion," 551.

[8] Ibid., 556.

[9] In November 1997, the NIJ renaned the DUF program as the Arrestee Drug Abuse Monitoring Programs (ADAM).

[10] Judy Reardon, "The Drug Use Forecasting Program: Measuring Drug Use in a Hidden Population," [http://health.state.ar.us/adaps/bbsfiles/duf.html], 21 May 1998, 11,18.

of offences. Consequently, only about 25% of participators have been charged with drug offenses.[11]

DUF was established when crack cocaine was becoming prominent in the nation. Prior to crack's appearance, however, results of two NIJ-funded drug testing research studies in Washing, D.C. and Manhattan, New York, indicated that a problem with cocaine probably was imminent. In March 1984, the NIJ awarded grants to the Washington, D.C. Pretrial Services agency (PSA) and to Narcotic and Drug Research, Inc. (NDRI), of New York City to use a newly developed test to screen for drugs through urinalysis.[12] The drug tests would be used to monitor the behavior of arrested persons released to the community prior to trial. Researchers found that participants tested positive for opiates,[13] cocaine, and PCP. Significantly in April 1984, 15% of arrestees tested positive for cocaine use, but by November 1984, the cocaine uses rates had grown to 22%, while the other drug use rates had slightly declined (opiates declined from about 21% to about 18%, and PCP from about 31% to about 29%).[14] Those outcomes prompted PSA Director Jay Carver to write a letter of warning on December 11, 1984, to the Chief Judge of the D.C. Superior court that a new drug, i.e., cocaine, outbreak might be on the horizon, similar to a heroin epidemic that occurred in the District in the 1970's. He stated that the cocaine use detected in persons arrested would eventually be noted in systems that monitored persons admitted to emergency rooms for drug-related problems and drug abuse treatment programs.[15] According to one source, no definitive response was received.[16]

Between April and October 1984, NDRI researchers in Manhattan conducted interviews and took urine samples from arrestees charged with nondrug felony offenses at the Manhattan Central Booking facility. Investigators tested for cocaine, opiates, methadone, and PCP. Results showed that of a total of 4,847 persons tested, 42% tested positive for cocaine, 21% for opiates, 12% for PCP, and 8% for methadone.[17]

---

[11] Eric D. Wish, "Drug Use Forecasting Program (DUF)," in *Encyclopedia of Drugs and Alcohol*, vol. 1, ed. Jerome H. Jaffe (New York: Simon & Schuster Macmillan, 1995), 434.

[12] Eric D. Wish, "The Crack Epidemic of the 1980's and the Birth of a New Drug Monitoring System in the United States," (paper presented at the conference on "The Crack Decade: Research Perspectives and Lessons Learned," cohosted by the National Institute of Justice and the National Institute on Drug Abuse, Baltimore, MD, November 4-5, 1997), 3-4.

[13] Opiates refer to any natural drug, rather than synthetic, that has properties similar to opium or morphine, its main active ingredient. McKim, *Drugs and Behavior,* 227.

[14] Wish, "The Crack Epidemic of the 1980's," 4, and Figure 2.

[15] Ibid., 4.

[16] Wish, telephone conversation with author, 20 May 1998.

[17] Ibid., 5.

In 1986, the NIJ awarded two grants to update and compare the 1984 findings. Results from the District's study showed that arrestees testing positive for cocaine had risen from 15% in April 1984 to 37% in April 1986.[18] In New York, twice as many arrestees testedpositive for cocaine in 1986 as those tested in 1984, i.e., 83% as compared with 42%. In November 1986, however, cocaine use dropped to 68%[19] among those tested, a change that was attributed to possible differences in the type of people arrested during that period. Use for all other drugs in this population remained stable.[20] No distinction could be made through urine samples between cocaine powder and crack cocaine use.

Noting that crack cocaine use was becoming prominent in 1986, particularly in New York, it could be assumed that the increase in cocaine use among arrestees reflected the growing use of crack cocaine. In 1986, the researchers observed, 70% of the arrestees who reported that they used cocaine indicated that they preferred to snort or smoke the drug.[21] Table 8 shows the 1984/1986 comparisons in cocaine use discovered through urinalysis of arrestees in New York City.

**Table 8. Comparison of Urine Tests Results For
Arrestees in Manhattan, 1984 and 1986**

Tested Positive For	Arrestees in 1984 (n = 4,847)*	Arrestees in Sept. & Oct. 1986 (n = 414)	Arrestees in Nov. 1986 (n = 201)
Cocaine	42%	83%	68%
Opiates	21%	22%	20%
Methadone	8%	8%	10%
PCP	12%	4%	3%
Any of the Above	56%	85%	73%
2+ of Above	23%	30%	23%

Source: the information appears as Table 3 in the article by Eric D. Wish, "Drug Use Forecasting: New York 1984 to 1986," *National Institute of Justice: Research in Action,* February 1987, 2.
*n = Total number of arrestees tested.

---

[18] Ibid.
[19] Ibid.
[20] Eric D. Wish, "Drug Use Forecasting: New York 1984 to 1986," *National Institute of Justice: Research in Action,* February 1987, 2.
[21] Wish, "The Crack Epidemic of the 1980's," 5.

At the start of the DUF program in early 1987, eight cities used it.[22] By November, the number had expanded to 12 cities that were chosen to represent various urban regions in the nation.[23] DUF data indicated that between June and November 1987, cocaine was the dominant drug used by arrestees in the 12 major cities, compared with other drugs tested for.[24] (See **Table 9**).

Table 9. DUF cities Reporting Positive Test Results for Any Drug Compared with Cocaine (Male Arrestees, June-November 1987), in Percentages

City	Testing Positive for Any Drug	Testing Positive for Cocaine
New York	79	63
Washington, D.C.	77	52
Fort Lauderdale	65	46
Detroit	66	53
Indianapolis	60	11
Chicago	73	50
New Orleans	72	45
Houston	62	43
Phoenix	53	21
Portland, Oregon	70	31
San Diego	75	44
Los Angeles	69	47

Source: Adapted from DUF bar graphs for January 1998 obtained from the National Institute of Justice.

These regional DUF data, recorded for a six-month period within 48 hours of arrest, far surpassed drug use statistics representing national level use of the mainstream population within the previous year, reported by the national household survey, NHDSA; or daily cocaine freebase, cocaine, or crack use within the last 30-days, lifetime, as well as use within the last year by high school seniors, via the NHSSS.

---

[22] Mieczkowski, "The Prevalence of Drug Use in the United States," 388.

[23] "Attorney General Announces NIJ Drug Use Forecasting System," *National Institute of Justice: Research in Action,* SNI 208, March/April 1988, 1.

[24] The drugs DUF analysts tested for were cocaine, marijuana, amphetamines, opiates, and PCP.

The DUF program has been called the "best measure of drug use among the criminal population."[25] Also, according to one drug abuse analyst, the pilot drug testing programs, forerunners of DUF and conducted in Washing, D.C. and Manhattan, New York, indicated a cocaine "epidemic" much earlier than the NHDSA or DAWN surveys.[26] A household survey researcher was reported as stating that DUF is not representative of anything because the data cannot be projected to any population because of the manner in which they are collected.[27] The GAO drug use measurement study stated, however, that DUF was not designed to measure national drug use rates of arrestees, but to assist local-level policy development and intervention programs. One particular strength DUF had over NHSDA and NHSSS, GAO noted, a strength that could be used to further local efforts, was that DUF did not rely solely on self-reported drug use of participants. Urinalysis results uncovered wide discrepancies between its findings and self-reports. This indicated that participants interviewed were not always truthful about drug use which might be substantially underreported, especially among arrestees.[28]

On the other hand, GAO commented that "methodological limitations" compromised the overall usefulness of the DUF program. For example, DUF listed names of participating cities in its publications, but data did not always represent arrestee drug use in the entire city – they could reflect parts of a city, county, or an entire county. That raised validity questions, the report stated, about the degree to which partial-area findings could be extrapolated to an entire city or county, and to what degree policy or programs based on limited data could be developed for a particular area.[29] GAO reported that NIJ officials disagreed with finding about the ability to generalize DUF data. NIJ administrators believed that a DUF sample could represent larger groups of arrestees booked for serious crimes in certain cities that use DUF.[30]

Another problem with DUF that GAO discovered was that uniform standards used in collecting data from arrestees were not applied in all cities using the program. That practice, GAO indicated, could limit data comparisons between cities and between males and females and could cause biased results.[31] NIJ managers took issue with that observation and

---

[25] Leen, "Number Jumble Clouds Judgement of Drug War," A20.

[26] Eric Wish, telephone conversation with author, 28 May 1998.

[27] Leen, "Number Jumble Clouds Judgement of Drug War," A20.

[28] General Accounting Office, *Drug Abuse Measurement*, 57.

[29] Ibid., 51.

[30] Ibid., 70.

[31] Ibid., 71.

contended that uniform standards in methodology across all participating sites were not important, because DUF's main purpose had been to collect useful data for local law enforcement agencies.[32]

Despite those limitations, DUF data appeared to indicate an increasingly serious cocaine abuse problem among persons arrested in large cities, one of the high risk groups missing from the other drug abuse measures. Notably, prior to and during the initial states of crack cocaine abuse in large U.S. cities, pre-DUF pilot drug testing program data indicated an imminent cocaine problem among arrestees that could have been an indicator of possible future problems for the nation.

Because of the reported strengths and weaknesses related to these various data sources between 1986 and 1988, when crack cocaine abuse became prominent in the United States, the true extent of that abuse could not be accurately determined. NHSDA and NHSSS measures might have dramatically understated the problem. GAO concluded,

> Since NHSDA and NHSSS do not sufficiently measure drug use among high-risk target groups, supplementary methods must be conceptualized, field-tested, and implemented if we are to better understand the drug prevalence rates and trends among these groups.[33]

Furthermore, although DAWN data, which was the only such indicator that depicted a serious problem with smokable cocaine abuse among the 18-years-and –older population (because of dramatic increased in cocaine-related medical emergencies) those data showed a sharper increase for persons who used "other" and "unknown" routes of administering the drug from 1985 to 1988. DAWN statistics could not be used to clearly measure the nationwide extent of crack cocaine use. The reason was because no relationship between cocaine-related medical emergencies and general use was determined. They did, however, reflect a major problem among cocaine abusers who suffered health hazards. Similarly, because of the DUF program's design for use only at local levels, it could not be used to extrapolate national crack cocaine use, but notable increases in cocaine use among arrestees indicated an escalating use of the drug within that high-risk population in the participating cities. Therefore, the initial nationwide magnitude of the crack cocaine problem among the mainstream population or high-risk groups cannot be accurately ascertained. The data that were available, however, did not indicate an extensive problem among the

---

[32] Ibid.
[33] Ibid., 65.

mainstream groups. A serious problem, however, appeared to be occurring among persons reporting to DAWN-participating hospital emergency rooms and the arrestees monitored by the DUF program.

Chapter 7

CONGRESSIONAL AND EXECUTIVE RESPONSE TO THE COCAINE PROBLEM

An in-depth explanation of how federal officials responded to the crack cocaine problem goes beyond the scope of this report. The General Accounting Office examines this topic in a report entitled, *Emerging Drug Problems: Despite Changes in Detection and Response Capability, Concerns Remain* (GAO/HEHS-98-130). This CRS report, however, presents an overview examining how Congress was made aware of a possible smokable-cocaine problem, and how they responded. Also discussed are certain executive branch activities in response to the nation's drug abuse problem and particularly to crack cocaine abuse.

CONGRESSIONAL AWARENESS OF AND RESPONSE TO CRACK COCAINE ABUSE

In 1979, at hearings before the House Select Committee on Narcotics Abuse and Control (see pp. 13 – 14), Dr. Robert Byck of the Yale University Medical School had warned Congress about a possible national problem with smokable cocaine abuse. He emphasized the need for research to examine the dangers of smoking cocaine, and suggested possible preventative measures. Author Jill Jonnes reported that years later, in 1995, Dr. Byck stated that he believed that no one "got the point."[1] The "point" that he attempted to convey was that smokable cocaine was highly addictive, that after initial use, most persons would quickly crave and seek to use the drug

---

[1] Jonnes, *Hep-Cats, Narcs, and Pipe Dreams,* 322.

again. A problem with the cocaine-smoking route of administration could be on the horizon in the nation if not quickly addressed. Dr. Byck mentioned to the Select Committee, however, that smokable cocaine was not yet a U.S. problem. That fact might have diminished an urgency for immediate action that Dr. Byck was attempting to convey.

Dr. David F. Musto, of the Yale University School of Medicine, observed in a 1997 presentation discussing "America's Experience With Drugs" (at a conference sponsored by NIDA and the National Institute of Justice) that a "warning" is complex. "It is difficult to pick out the valid warning," he stated, "difficult to get anyone to pay attention to the warning even if valid, and difficult to decide what is the best response."[2] The House Select Committee had been warned about smokable cocaine and therefore was aware of the concern. Its response to the warnings, as well as that of other Members of Congress who might have had some related concerns about illicit drugs, is a means of assessing whether or not Congress appeared to clearly understand the message.

Congress responded to public and medical concerns about cocaine by holding several hearings to assess the drug and its impact on society. Subsequently, it passed legislation (discussed below) to control illicit drug trafficking and the use of illegal drugs in society. The more significant of those activities, which in some cases singled out cocaine and eventually crack cocaine, are discussed below.

Cocaine-Related Congressional Hearings and Smokable-Cocaine Concerns

In 1979, the House Select Committee held five cocaine-related hearings. The initial warnings about smokable cocaine were given at the first two hearings held on July 24 and 26. On October 10, 1979, the third hearing was conducted to determine cocaine's cost to society in terms of its negative impact on people's lives and the expense of law enforcement efforts. Kevin E. McEneaney, Director of Public Information for the Phoenix House Foundation, which operated a residential drug treatment program, testified, among other witnesses. Mr. McEneaney was in charge of Drug Prevention Education programs that were presented annually in schools and

---

[2] David F. Musto, "America's Experience With Drugs," presented to "The Crack Decade: Research Perspectives and Lessons Learned," National Institute on Drug Abuse and the National Institute of Justice, (4 November 1997), 26.

communities across the nation. While explaining the negative impact cocaine could have on users, particularly young users, he stated,

> I'm sure the committee has heard enough expert testimony on the physical effects of cocaine and the particular danger of smoking the drug in the form of coca paste or free-base cocaine. So let me move onto what we have learned about young users now in Phoenix House ...[C]hemical kits to convert street cocaine to free-base are available through the Nation's huge headshop net. So we can expect to see the same extreme examples of dependency and the same psychological symptoms that researchers have reported among coke smokers in South America.[3]

Drug Paraphernalia Hearings and Smokable Cocaine

A related issue that became evident during the October hearing was that drug paraphernalia sold at head shops (which basically were retail stores that sold apparatus for illicit drug use) contributed to the glamorization of the drug trade, particularly cocaine. Hearing testimony revealed information about cocaine freebasing and other drug use could be obtained through the drug paraphernalia industry head shops.[4] Congress held two hearings in November 1979 to examine the drug paraphernalia industry. The first by the U.S. House Select Committee on Narcotics abuse and Control occurred on November 1[5] and the second, by the U.S. Senate committee on the Judiciary's subcommittee on Criminal Justice, on November 16.[6]

The House Select Committee met to " assess the impact of advertising and unregulated sale of drug paraphernalia upon drug abuse, particularly among...youth, and to consider governmental initiatives to exercise control over the paraphernalia industry."[7] Sue Rusche, a spokesman for a parental organization in Atlanta, Georgia, testified, as well as representatives for Phoenix House, the DEA, police departments and the drug paraphernalia industry.

---

[3] House Select Committee, *Cocaine: A Major Drug Issue of the Seventies*, 124.

[4] Ibid., 118-199.

[5] House Select Committee on Narcotics Abuse and Control, *Drug Paraphernalia: Hearing*, 96th Cong., 1st Sess., 1 November 1979.

[6] Senate Committee on the Judiciary, Subcommittee on Criminal Justice, *Drug Paraphernalia and Youth: Hearing before the Subcommittee on Criminal Justice*, 96th Cong., 2nd sess., 1980, Committee Print SCNAC-96-1-6, 1.

[7] House Select Committee on Narcotics Abuse and Control, *Drug Paraphernalia*, 96th Cong., 2nd sess., 1980, Committee Print SCNAC-96-1-6, 1.

A significant presentation at the hearing was made by Dr. S. Franklin Sher, a family physician, surgeon, and forensic toxicologist who had practiced in the San Francisco Bay area for 22 years. Dr. Sher discussed the effects of smoking freebase cocaine and the ease of converting cocaine powder into smokable freebase form by using apparatus contained in conversion kits. The kits could be purchased at drug paraphernalia head shops. Dr. Sher provided a conversion kit for the select Committee to examine.

Dr. Sher was asked to respond to the July hearing statements of Dr. Byck and Dr. Peterson warning about the dangers of smokable cocaine.[8] He stated that he disagreed with Dr. Byck regarding the harmful effects of smokable cocaine. He based his conclusion on personal interviews with people who had smoked cocaine freebase over a long period of time and had not experienced adverse effects.[9] The Select Committee now had two opinions to consider concerning the health effects of smokable cocaine – one based on scientific studies plus the personal examination of patients in Peru who had smoked coca paste, and the other based on personal interviews. Focused at that time on the impact of the drug paraphernalia industry on society, the House Select Committee conducted its own investigation to examine the drug apparatus problem.

It determined tht the unregulated sale and advertising of drug paraphernalia encouraged drug abuse and experimentation by children and youth, and promoted the general public's acceptance of illicit drug use. Consequently, the Select Committee felt that government regulation was required and recommended that state and local governments strongly consider enacting laws similar to the DEA's Model Drug Paraphernalia Act (a guide to state and local governments for legislative proposals and laws to address the drug paraphernalia concern). Furthermore, the Select Committee urged that state and local governments consider enacting laws prohibiting the sale of drug paraphernalia to minors, and limit the commercial area where such products could be sold. In addition, it suggested that the U.S. Attorney General quickly review ingestible drugs and/or substances advertised in "prodrug" publications and sold by paraphernalia stores to decide whether such activities could be potentially abusive and should be scheduled under the Control Substances Act of 1970 (P.L. 91-513). Lastly, the Select Committee urged state and local governments to take immediate action to

---

[8] House Select Committee Hearing, *Drug Paraphernalia*, 48.
[9] Ibid., 59.

prohibit the advertising and sale of drug paraphernalia that enabled users to consume or ingest controlled substances while operating a motor vehicle.[10]

On November 16, the Senate Committee on the Judiciary's Subcommittee on Criminal Justice held a hearing in Baltimore, Maryland, to examine the concerns about drug paraphernalia. The forum was to be the first in a series of planned hearings in cities away from Washington, D.C., to obtain citizen input about the paraphernalia problem. A panel of concerned parents testified, as did other citizens who were against drug paraphernalia because of its perceived negative influence on children. They urged Congress to enact legislation that would ban the sell of drug paraphernalia in head shops, which in many instances reportedly were located near elementary and/or secondary schools.[11] Paraphernalia industry representative Kenneth M. Bombard of the Mid-Atlantic Accessories Trade association (MATA) denied that the drug paraphernalia industry negatively influenced children, and recommended along with other MATA spokesman that effective drug education programs be created for children in schools and communities.[12]

These congressional actions and individual state activities contributed to the eventual demise of the drug paraphernalia industry. Although by the end of 1981, many states had enacted anti-drug paraphernalia legislation that was influenced by the Model Drug Paraphernalia Act, there were some states where such laws had not been enacted and drug paraphernalia availability through mail-order prompted further actions by the U.S. Congress. The "Mail Order Drug Paraphernalia Control Act of 1986" (H.R. 1625) was inserted as Subtitle O, "Prohibition on the Interstate Sale and Transportation of Drug Paraphernalia," into Title I, "Anti-Drug Enforcement," of the Anti-Drug Abuse Act of 1986. The Act became Public Law 99-570 on October 27, 1986. Later, on November 29, 1990, the Crime Control Act was signed into law (P.L. 101-647), amending the Controlled Substances Act of 1970 (P.L. 91-513) by transferring Title I, Subtitle O, "Drug Paraphernalia," to Title II, Section 422 of the Control Substances Act. That provision prohibited any person from selling, offering for sale, and using the mails or any other facility of interstate commerce to transport, import, or export drug paraphernalia.

By 1988, 49 states and the District of Columbia (DC) had sought to control the sale of drug paraphernalia through state laws or local ordinances. Furthermore, 39 of those states and DC enacted statutes based on the DEA

---

[10] House Select Committee Print, *Drug Paraphernalia,* 1.

[11] Senate Committee on the Judiciary, *Drug Paraphernalia and Youth,* 44, 58, 62.

Model Drug Paraphernalia Act.[13] Through those actions, the drug paraphernalia industry basically was driven underground.

Drug-Abuse-Related Hearings and Landmark Anti-Drug-Abuse Legislation and Its Impact on Crack Cocaine

In September 1980, the House Select Committee on Narcotics Abuse and Control held hearings to review the status of the federal efforts to prevent and control drug abuse and drug trafficking in the nation as well as abroad. Witnesses were urged to provide information about the most critical drug abuse issues the nation might face in the 1980's and how Congress should be better equipped to assist with efforts to prevent and control drug abuse.[14] NIDA Director William Pollin, one of many federal officials who testified, stated that, in spite of a "first-time" leveling off of nationwide use of all illicit drugs, he believed that drug abuse was a national public health problem that would worsen in the 1980's. Also he stated, "there is every likelihood, almost a certainty, that the pace of development of new drugs, more potent drugs, will continue to accelerate during the coming decade."[15] Furthermore, he and others who testified, such as Dr. Lee Dogoloff, associate Director of the White House Domestic Policy Staff, believed that drug abuse prevention programs should be stressed to head off any future drug abuse problems.[16]

Select Committee Chairman, Representative Lester L. Wolff, stressed the Select Committee's belief that the highest national priority should be given toward efforts to prevent drug abuse and drug trafficking. Also, because the Select Committee was due to expire at the end of the year, committee members recommended to the House leadership that a permanent oversight committee be created to assure that a comprehensive effort to develop sound public policy for drug control would continue.[17]

The House passed legislation that allowed the Select Committee to continue to operate throughout the 1980's. Numerous hearings were held exploring drug-abuse-related concerns. Various Members of Congress

---

[12] Ibid., 108.

[13] Department of Justice, National Institute of Justice, Office of Communication and Research Utilization, *State and Local Experience with Drug Paraphernalia Laws*, by Kerry Murphy Healy (1988), 1.

[14] House Select Committee, *Federal Drug Strategy*, 2.

[15] Ibid., 41.

[16] Ibid., 21, 43, 53.

[17] Ibid.

introduced legislation, much of which became law, to designate a specific "National Drug Abuse Education and Prevention Week," as well as a "Just Say No to Drugs Week," and when crack cocaine became prominent, a "Crack/Cocaine Awareness Month," also a "Drug Free America Week."[18] Certain significant occurrences during the decade (highlighted below) appeared to influence congressional response to drug abuse and particularly cocaine and, eventually, crack cocaine abuse.

In 1982, President Ronald declared "war" on the drug trade. In 1983, the House Committee on the Judiciary held hearings to assess drug production and trafficking in Latin America and in the Carribean and the impact of the availability of illicit drugs, including cocaine in the nation. In 1984, Congress enacted legislation that became Public Law 98-473, the Comprehensive Crime Control Act of 1984. This law, which created the U.S. Sentencing Commission to produce mandatory sentencing, also included mandatory minimum penalties for drug trafficking offenses and abolished parole for persons convicted under the guidelines.[19]

On July 16, 1985, the House select committee held a hearing to report to the nation about the "ever-increasing danger of a cocaine epidemic" that was sweeping the nation. The Select Committee chairman, Representative Charles Rangel, reported that cocaine-related deaths had grown sharply, from 192 between 1979 and 1980 to 456 between 1983 and 1984.[20]

An over supply of cocaine in Peru, Bolivia, and Chile lowered cocaine prices, which caused the demand to increase markedly. That situation was believed by some commentators to have contributed to the rise of crack. Appearing first in late 1985, reports about crack as a new drug menace were common in the media by mid- 1986. On June 19, 1986, Len Bias, a University of Maryland basketball star who had been drafted to play for the Boston Celtics the day before, died from a cocaine overdose. That incident seemed to produce a change in the nation's response toward cocaine abuse. The U.S. Sentencing Commission (USSC) stated in its February 1995 report

---

[18] Some of the laws designating "National Drug Abuse Education Week" and some including both "Drug Education and Prevention" in the titles were P.L. 98-142 (11/01/83), P.L. 98-385 (08/21/84), P.L. 99-143 (11/07/85), P.L. 99-407 (08/27/86), and P.L. 99-446 (10/06/86). P.L. 99-309 (05/20/86), P.L. 100-37 (05/12/87), and P.L. 100-313 (05/10/88) designated "Just Say No to Drugs Week," P.L. 99-481 (10/16/86) designated October 1986 "Crack/Cocaine Awareness Month," and P.L. 100-455 (09/29/88) designated a "Drug Free America Week."

[19] "The National Legislative and Law Enforcement Response to Cocaine," In United States Sentencing Commission, *Special Report to the Congress: Cocaine and Federal Sentencing Policy*, February 1995,[http://www.ussc.gov/crack/EXEC.HTM].

[20] House Select Committee on Narcotics Abuse and Control, *Cocaine Abuse and the Federal Response: Hearing*, 99th Cong., 1st Sess., 16 July 1985, 1.

to Congress that the method of cocaine ingestion that killed Bias was not initially known. Newspapers across the country, however, quoted Dr. Dennis Smyth, Maryland's Assistant Medical Examiner, as attributing it to cocaine freebase because of the high levels of cocaine in Bias's bloodstream.[21] Although, Maryland's Chief Medical Examiner, Dr. John Smialek, stated that the death was due to snorting cocaine powder and not to cocaine freebasing, the bulk of the media coverage attributed it to crack.[22]

A few weeks after Bias's death, two simultaneous congressional hearings were held on July 15, 1986 (a joint hearing of the House Select Committee on Narcotics Abuse and Control and the Select Committee on Children, Youth, and Families, plus a hearing by the Senate Committee on Government Affairs Permanent Subcommittee on Investigations) that explored concerns about crack cocaine abuse.[23] During the Senate Subcommittee discussions, the USSC report states, Len Bias's death was mentioned repeatedly. Additionally, the USSC study indicated that Bias's death influenced the development of federal crack cocaine laws and Congress's decision to differentiate crack cocaine from powder cocaine in the penalty structure of the landmark legislation, The Anti-Drug Abuse Act of 1986 (P.L. 99-570), signed into law nearly three and one-half months later, on October 27, 1986.[24] The USSC study further stated that floor statements by certain Members of Congress indicated that (1) Congress had concluded that crack cocaine was more dangerous than powder cocaine, and (2) that conclusion drove its decision to treat crack cocaine differently than cocaine powder,[25] Specifically, persons convicted for distributing one pound of powder cocaine would be sentenced to fewer years in federal prison than a person convicted of distributing five grams or more of crack cocaine.[26]

In addition to legislating stiff sentencing penalties for distributing crack cocaine, and encouraging international narcotics control activities, the Anti-Drug Abuse Act of 1986 also advocated the creation of effective drug abuse prevention and education programs, and the expansion of federal support for

---

[21] "The National Legislative and Law Enforcement Response to Cocaine" [http://www.ussc. gov/crack/chap6.htm.].

[22] Ibid.

[23] House Select Committee on Narcotics Abuse and Control, and the Select Committee on Children, Youth, and Families, *The Crack Cocaine Crisis.*
Senate Committee on governmental Affairs, permanent subcommittee on Investigations, *"Crack" Cocaine: Hearing,* 99th Cong., 2nd Sess., 15 July 1986.

[24] "The National Legislative and Law Enforcement Response to Cocaine," [http://www.ussc. gov/crack/chap6.htm].

[25] Ibid.

[26] Congressional Research Service, *Federal Cocaine Sentencing: Legal Issues,* by Paul S. Wallace, Jr., CRS Report 97-743, 28 July 1997,1.

drug abuse treatment and rehabilitation efforts.[27] This aspect of the law represented the first time an active federal role in drug abuse education and prevention had been established.[28] One of the major concerns of policymakers and administrators regarding the implementation of the act was the adequacy of federal funding for the programs - $200 million for FY 1987, $250 million for FY 1988, and $250 million for FY 1989 for a variety of drug abuse education and prevention programs.[29] In comparison, a total of $241 million was allotted for treatment, rehabilitation, and research,[30] while $296 million was authorized for federal domestic drug law enforcement activities to discourage national drug trafficking and drug use, and $575 million for national drug interdiction activities to deter drug smugglers from entering the nation at its borders.[31] Clearly, the law enforcement efforts apeared to be highlighted more than the education, prevention, research, rehabilitation and treatment activities.

On November 18, 1988, the Anti-Drug Abuse Act of 1988 became Public Law 100-690. The legislation created the Office of National Drug Control Policy (ONDCP) in the Executive Office of the President. ONDCP was mandated to create policies, precedent, and goals for the national drug control program.[32] The objectives of the drug control programs were to "reduce illicit drug use, manufacturing and trafficking, drug-related crime and violence, and drug-related health consequences."[33] The Director of the ONDCP (popularly called the "drug czar") would provide an annual National Drug Control Strategy which the President would submit to Congress; direct the nation's drug abuse efforts; and create program, budget, and policy guidelines for cooperative tasks among federal, state, and local entities.[34]

Compared with the 1986 mandate, the 1988 anti-drug-abuse law placed increased emphasis on treatment and prevention by creating the Office of Substance Abuse Prevention (authorizing $95 million for FY 1989 and sums as necessary for the succeeding fiscal years 1990 and 1991).[35] OSAP would

---

[27] P.L. 99-570, 100 Stat. 3207.

[28] House Select Committee on Narcotics Abuse and Control, *Implementation of the Anti-Drug Abuse Act of 1986,* 100th Cong., 1st Sess., 1988, Committee Print, 6.

[29] Ibid.

[30] Ibid., 7.

[31] Ibid., 25.

[32] Office of National Drug Control Policy, Purpose, [http://www.whitehousedugpolicy.gov/ about/purpose.html]. No date.

[33] Ibid.

[34] Ibid.

[35] P.L. 100-690, sec. 2051 (a), 102 Stat. 4206.

provide training for clinical personnel and other health professional involved in drug abuse education, prevention, and intervention; provide community assistance in developing comprehensive long-term strategies for substance abuse prevention; and evaluate the community programs. The law authorized $75 million for an FY 1989 program to reduce the waiting period for drug abuse treatment,[36] and provided programs to assist at-risk youth. Also, $23 million was authorized for national drug interdiction activities,[37] and $275 million for state and local law enforcement agencies.[38] The death penalty culd be invoked for any drug trafficker who murdered someone during a drug-related crime, or for anyone who killed a law enforcement officer in such an incident.[39] Congress appropriated only $500 million to address the entire dug abuse problem because of the FY1989 balanced-budget requirements of the Gramm-Rudman-Hollings Act of 1985.[40]

The general nature of the anti-drug-abuse legislation seemed to be driven by awareness of the crack cocaine problem that had been heightened by the media especially in 1986. One commentator observed that several investigators believed that the response by the media and politicians appeared to have been well out of proportion to the actual extent and seriousness of the crack cocaine problem.[41] The USSC study stated that Congress's conclusions about the dangerousness of crack were based on the assumptions that it was more addictive than cocaine powder, there was a greater correlation between crack use and crime than with other drugs, crack use could lead to psychosis and death, young people were more prone to use crack, and its ease of manufacture, use, purity and potency would lead to widespread national use.[42] Although scientific research results available in 1986 did indicate that cocaine-freebase smokers did tend to have an intense

---

[36] "increased federal Funds for Treatment," by Edward Klebe, in Congressional Research Service, *National Drug Control Strategy, 1989: Background and Policy Questions,* coordinated by Harry Hogan, CRS Report 89-567 GOV, 29 September 1989, 21.

[37] "Tactical Intelligence Gathering and Analysis," by Harry Hogan, in Congressional Research Service, *National Drug Control Strategy, 1989,* 46.

[38] *"Grants for State and Local Drug Law Enforcement",* by Kieth Bea, in Congressional Research Service, *National Drug Strategy,* 5.

[39] Charles Culhane, "Congress Says Yes to Drug Bill," 19.

[40] Charles Culhane, "Congress Says Yes to Drug Bill," *The U.S. Journal of Drug and Alcohol Dependence,* 12 (November 1988), 1.
The Balanced Budget and Emergency Deficit Control Act of 1985 (P.L. 99-177), popularly known as the Gramm-Rudman-Hollings Act, was enacted to incrementally reduce the federal budget deficit to zero by FY 1991.

[41] Steve R. Blenko, *Crack and the Evolution of Anti-Drug Policy,* (Westport, Connecticut: Greenwood Press, 1993), 13.

[42] "The National Legislative and Law Enforcement Response to Cocaine," [http://www.ussc.gov/crack/chap6.htm]. no date.

craving for the drug (see Appendix 1), there was not enough scientific research about crack use per se, nor accurate prevalence data available, to confirm those beliefs.

The ONDCP was scheduled to terminate on September 30, 1997 almost 10 years after the Anti-Drug Abuse Act of 1988 was enacted. Congress, however, approved funding for the office to continue operating through the passage of the Treasury Department FY 1998 Appropriations bill, (P.L. 105-61) on October 10, 1997. On October 21, 1997, the House passed amended H.R. 2610, The National Narcotics Leadership Act, to reauthorize ONDCP. On November 6, 1997, the Senate Committee on the Judiciary favorably reported the measure (without written report) amended by substituting a new version of the bill, entitled, the Office of National Drug Control Policy Reauthorization Act.[43] No further action has occurred.

EXECUTIVE BRANCH RESPONSE TO DRUG ABUSE, PARTICULARLY COCAINE AND CRACK COCAINE ABUSE

On June 24, 1982 President Reagan declared a "War on Drugs." To enforce that activity which specifically focused on the drug trade, he established the White House Office of Drug Abuse Policy. Those actions were taken nearly five months after he had created a south Florida Task Force on January 28, 1982, to make a concentrated federal effort to stop South American smugglers from importing cocaine into the nation. Vice President George Bush was selected to oversee the effort, the goal of which was to stop drugs from entering the United States. [44]

Also in 1982, "Just Say No," a slogan associated with First Lady Nancy Reagan, became what has been termed a "rallying cry" for the nation to prevent drug abuse among the youth.[45] Furthermore, NIDA, the primary federal public health agency with the mission to monitor the nature and extent of national drug abuse and develop prevention programs to assist youth, began, through its Communications Services Branch (later renamed

---

[43] Congressional Research Service, *Drug Control: Reauthorization of the Office of National Drug Control Policy,* by David Teasley, CRS Report 98-149, 4 May 1998, 1. See this report for detailed information about the re-authorization of ONDCP.

[44] Isikoff, "Drug Wars Past and Present," A17.

[45] Avraham forman and Susan B. Lachter, "The National Institute on Drug Abuse Cocaine Prevention Campaign," in *Communication Campaigns About Drugs,* ed. Pamela J. Shoemaker, 15.

the Office for Research Communications), extensive media efforts to discourage drug abuse among young teenagers called "The Just Say No" campaign. That endeavor set the groundwork for the planning of a national media cocaine-prevention campaign that began in June 1984.[46] Based on scientific research results about the serious social and health consequences of cocaine, the "multimedia" cocaine-abuse prevention campaign was developed and entitled, "Cocaine: The Big Lie." It targeted older teenagers and young adults, 18 to 35 years of age, who were thought to be the largest group of cocaine abusers. The campaign attempted to deglamorize the drug by presenting credible and useful information that would attract and reach that audience.[47] Those efforts were launched just prior to the emergence of crack cocaine on the national scene.

In April 1986, the first of 13 televised public service announcements about the hazards of cocaine use began in 75 local television markets. Those television markets aired the spots 1,500 to 2,500 times per month.[48] NIDA considered the campaign to be successful because of its timeliness and the quality of the public service announcements.[49] "By the summer of 1986," NIDA officials reported, "cocaine was an important item on the national agenda." Furthermore, they believed, "in addition to the NIDA campaign, the tragic death from a cocaine overdose of University of Maryland basketball star Len Bias, the continuing revelations of cocaine use by professional athletes, and the advent of crack cocaine focused intense media and governmental attention on cocaine abuse during the last half of that year."[50]

Despite those executive branch drug-abuse-related activities, on July 15, 1986, Representative Charles Rangel, Chairman of the House Select Committee on Narcotics Abuse and Control, in his opening statement at the joint hearing convened to discuss the widespread use of crack cocaine, stated that he believed the nation was losing in the effort to save children and young people from the devastation of drug use.[51] Furthermore, he commented that no portion of the war-on-drugs effort was properly funded at the federal level. This situation, he said, hampered local level efforts in

---

[46] Ibid., 14-15.
[47] Ibid., 13.
[48] Ibid., 17.
[49] Ibid.
[50] Ibid., 17, 19.
[51] House Select Committees, *The Crack Cocaine Crisis: Joint Hearing,* 1.

meeting the demand of those who sought rehabilitation, avoidance of drug use, or who were in trouble because of drug use.[52]

A statement by Jesse Brewer, Deputy Chief of police in south-central Los Angeles and who also was a member of President Reagan's Commision on Organized Crime, appeared to corroborate Mr. Rangel'' concerns. Mr. Brewer'' comments were reported in an article appearing in the February 1985 issue of *The U.S. Journal of Drug and Alcohol Dependence* The article related that crack already was a problem for the 500,000 black residents in south-central Los Angeles.[53] Mr. Brewer remarked, "We're stretched to the limit. We need a cohesive plan including all agencies. All we are doing now is making the dealing less conspicuous. We have not put our money where our mouth is, and there is not enough concern among legislators. When it is apparent that this affects all of society, then we'll take action."[54] Mr. Brewer appeared to place the blame for the lack of a cohesive drug abuse prevention plan on legislators. Furthermore, no data source provided an accurate assessment of the crack cocaine situation at that time to corroborate Mr. Brewer's description of the severity of the problem.

In 1986, amidst what appeared to be the crack abuse crisis, the executive branch responded with NIDA's televised public service announcements to warn the public about the harmfulness of cocaine. On September 14, 1986, President Reagan and the first Lady spoke against the drug abuse menace, especially crack, during a nationally televised broadcast. The President reported that 37 federal agencies were working together in a vigorous national effort to control drug abuse. Cocaine, however, continued to be smuggled into the nation at alarming levels. He mentioned particularly "a new epidemic: smokable cocaine, otherwise known as crack," which he referred to as "an explosively destructive and often lethal substance which is crushing its users," and was "an uncontrolled fire."[55]

The First Lady cited her personal crusade to encourage young people to "just say no." To combat the drug problem, the President announced six initiatives that would become national goals through a combined government and private effort. They were (1) seeking drug-free workplaces, (2) seeking drug-free schools, (3) ensuring available treatment for substance abusers and the chemically dependent, (4) expanding international cooperation and

---

[52] Ibid., 2.

[53] Mike Ruppert, "New Epidemic: 'Rock' Cocaine Hits L.A.," *The U.S. Journal of Drug and Alcohol Dependence*, 9 (February 1985): 1, 4.

[54] Ibid., 4.

treating drug trafficking as a national security threat, (5) strengthening law enforcement activities, and (6) seeking to expand public awareness and prevention.[56] Together with ongoing efforts, those proposals, he announced, would bring the federal commitment to fighting drugs to $3 billion.[57]

On September 15, 1986, the day after the televised broadcast, the President submitted to Congress the "Drug-Free America Act of 1986," requesting immediate consideration and enactment of legislation that he hoped would become the cornerstone of the Administration's antidrug efforts.[58] The proposal contributed to what became an omnibus anti-drug-abuse bill, the Anti-Drug Abuse Act of 1986, that the President signed into law in October, authorizing nearly $1.7 billion to reduce drug and alcohol abuse.[59]

On March 26, 1987, by Executive Order 12590, President Reagan created the National Drug Policy Board originally created under the Crime Control Act of 1984 as the National Drug Enforcement Policy Board. Chaired by the Attorney General, the Board was directed to facilitate and coordinate the national drug policy and integrate activities of executive departments and agencies to address the illegal drug abuse problem.[60] The executive order extended the Board's authority to include efforts to control the demand for drugs. To assist in facilitating the goal to control drug demand, the Secretary of Health and Human Services functioned as the board's Vice Chairman. The Anti-Drug Abuse Act of 1988 replaced the board with the Office of National Drug Control Policy (P.L. 100-690, Title I, Coordination of National Drug Policy, Subtitle A, Sec. 1002).[61]

In 1988, the last phase of NIDA's "Cocaine, The Big Lie," campaign began. It was designed to address crack-abusing teenagers and assist family members of cocaine abusers.[62] By that time, the DEA reported that crack

---

[55] "National Campaign Against Drug Abuse," Address to the Nation, September 14, 1986, in *Weekly Compilation of Presidential Documents, September 22, 1986*, vol. 22, no. 38, 1184.

[56] Ibid., 1185 – 1186.

[57] Ibid., 1186.

[58] Ibid., 1192 – 1193.

[59] Charles Culhane, "Legislative Photo Finish: $1.7 Billion Passed," *The U.S. Journal of Drug and Alcohol Dependence*, 10 (November 1986): 1.

[60] "National Drug Policy Board," Executive Order 12590, 26 March 1987, In *Weekly Compilation of Presidential Documents, March 30, 1987*, vol. 23, no. 12, 308.

[61] House Committee on Government Operations, *Drug Abuse and its Control: Glossary of Selected Terms*, report prepared by the Congressional Research Service of the Library of Congress, 101st Cong., 2nd sess., 1990, Committee Print, 61.

[62] "Cocaine: The Big Lie, 1986-1988," *NIDA Capsules*, National Institute on Drug Abuse Capsule Series C-88-02, The National Clearinghouse for Alcohol and Drug Information [http://www.health.org/pubs/caps/NCBigLie.htm]. No date.

abuse had appeared to permeate nearly every state in the nation and was considered to be a major medical problem.[63] As previously mentioned, no accurate data were available to corroborate that claim. Seemingly responding to this situation as assessed by the DEA, NIDA, in addition to providing the media spots, also set up a toll-free telephone drug-treatment referral line for callers to learn about cocaine use and its consequences, and to obtain information about local treatment programs. In its first year of operation, 1-800-662-HELP received over 50,000 calls.[64]

NIDA analysts concluded that the "Cocaine, The Big Lie" campaign was successful because of the heavy response to the referral hotline. There was no way of knowing, however, how many persons the campaign prevented from using cocaine.[65]

---

[63] Drug Enforcement Administration, *Crack Cocaine: Overview 1989*, 1.

[64] Forman and Lachter, "The National Institute on Drug Abuse Cocaine Prevention Campaign," 19.

[65] Ibid., 20.

Chapter 8

CONCLUSIONS AND OBSERVATIONS

Crack cocaine appeared on the national scene in late 1985. By early 1986, a crack cocaine crisis seemed to be developing among the older youth and adults. The crisis significantly escalated by early 1987. Whether there was a crack epidemic between 1986 and 1987 could not be proven and still is debatable. A lack of accurate incidence and prevalence data during the period the problem first appeared is the primary reason for the uncertainty. At a 1986 joint hearing of the House Select Committee on Narcotics Abuse and Control and the Select Committee on Children, Youth, and Families, Dr. Jerome H. Jaffe, Director of NIDA's Addiction Research Center, testified that its monitoring system, i.e., its household survey and other epidemiological techniques to gauge the extent and patterns of drug use, was missing a "recent wave of cocaine smoking affecting young people in some minority communities," but was believed to be reliable for the nation as a whole.[1] Furthermore, he stated, "Although our data systems are not seeing any substantial upturn in the number of cocaine users, analysis of these data does indicate those who are using cocaine are using more cocaine and using it more frequently."[2] Also, Dr. Jaffe indicated that he considered crack cocaine to be a serious crisis facing the nation at that time,[3] although the available data did not seem to indicate such a serious crisis.

Trend analysis of the 1988 National Household Survey data indicated a significant decline in the current (within the past month) use of illicit drugs between 1985 and 1988 among all categories – i.e., all age groups 12 and

---

[1] House Select Committee on Narcotics Abuse and Control, and the Select Committee on Children, Youth, and Families, *The Crack Cocaine Crisis,* 25.

[2] Ibid., 26.

[3] Ibid., 27.

older, in both men and women, by race and ethnic categories (black, white, and Hispanic), in all regions of the nation, and among all educational levels.[4] Nevertheless, most media accounts implied that crack cocaine abuse widely devastated society. One commentator observed that "the theme" of what he termed "the crack era" was that "drug abuse might destroy America if left unchecked…"[5] The same researcher, however, observed that media coverage of crack cocaine dissipated considerably in 1987. Further, he noticed that media coverage had a less urgent and sensationalistic tone after the 1986 elections which he believed were significantly connected with the media and federal officials' responses.[6] In addition, the analyst believed that although crack cocaine was a relatively serious drug with a high addiction potential, "the reaction of policy makers to its emergence was too overreaching and not in balance with the prevalence of crack use or its real effects on overall crime rates." Subsequently, a more realistic view about crack emerged but only after the media coverage about the problem declined.[7] Another observer remarked that "the media can mobilize public opinion, set trends of thought, even make discussion about formerly taboo subjects quite respectable… It also has the power to distort, to misalign our focus, [and] to disinform us."[8]

A 1988 study assessing the national climate in 1986 stated, "this was a period when the news media paid more attention to crack cocaine use and its health and criminal consequences."[9] The study concluded that since most American citizens had very little direct experience regarding the illicit drug problem, their views were shaped by the content and magnitude of the media coverage about the issue. Additionally, it was determined that "the public is likely to be swayed by what they see on weekly television health and crime drama series, by large paid-for-advertising campaigns, and by public service advertisements that espouse a particular drug policy viewpoint."[10] Although the true extent of the initial crack cocaine problem might never be resolved, one possible lesson from the experience is what appeared to be the strong role of the media in influencing public opinion about crack. Such influence might benefit ongoing public-education programs to keep current and

---

[4] "Highlights of the 1988 National Household Survey on Drug Abuse: National Institute on Drug Abuse," *NIDA Capsules*, C-86-13, Revised August 1989, 1.

[5] Belenko, *Crack and the Evolution of Anti-Drug Policy*, 3.

[6] Ibid., 25.

[7] Ibid., 7.

[8] Milan Korcok, "Television's Role in Drug Battle: Are We Getting the Whole Picture?" *The U.S. Journal of Drug and Alcohol Dependence*, 10 (October 1986): 7.

[9] Robert J. Blendon and John T. Young, "The Public and the War on Illicit Drugs," *JAMA.*, 279, 11 (18 March 1998): 828.

[10] Ibid., 831.

succeeding generations properly informed about the negative effects of drug use and abuse. Many observers believe that improved data collection could provide a more accurate measure of drug use and abuse leading to more specifically targeted anti-drug-abuse public education programs. NIDA analysts observed the following about drug abuse in the United States:

> The Historical data show that the absence of public education programs can often lead to a return to a tolerance of drug use as it did in the late 1970s. People need to be reminded about the social and health consequences of drug abuse as a key to a healthy society.[11]

Therefore, strengthening society's historical knowledge about past drug abuse occurrences in the United States and their outcomes also might be an effective method to maintain public awareness about the hazardous consequences of illicit drugs, and help diminish future problems. Knowledge about the nation's first cocaine crisis, which lasted from around 1885 to the 1920's according to David F. Musto of Yale University, was not transmitted to succeeding generations and basically was unknown to the masses after drug use sharply declined in the 1940's.[12]

What Dr. Musto refers to as "America's first great cocaine epidemic," had three phases – "the introduction during the 1880's, as cocaine rapidly gained acceptance; a middle period, when its use spread and its ill effects came to light; and a final, repressive stage after the turn of the century, when cocaine became the most feared of all illicit drugs."[13] These stages seem similar to the experience with cocaine since the 1970's, when its use again became prominent in the nation. By the late 1890's, Dr. Musto reported, cocaine, which had once been considered "the miracle drug of upper class professionals," had become known as a "curse." In 1909, an article by an antidrug activist warned that it was the most harmful of all habit-forming drugs. "As early as 1887," Musto reported, "the states had begun enacting their own (largely ineffective) laws against cocaine and other drugs."[14] In 1914, Congress passed the Harrison Act, which tightly regulated the distribution and sale of all illegal drugs. By 1917, and the U.S. entry into

---

[11] Lachter and Forman, "Drug Abuse in the United States," 11.

[12] David F. Musto, "America's first Cocaine Epidemic," *Wilson Quarterly*, 13 (Summer 1989): 60-62.

[13] Ibid., 60.

[14] Ibid., 63.

World War I, all 48 states had enacted anticocaine laws, and 14 states initiated "drug education" programs in public schools.[15]

Although some individuals continued to use the drug after 1917, Dr. Musto explained, their numbers eventually dwindles. Furthermore, he reported, "peer pressure and the threat of punishment combined to drive cocaine underground."[16] By the late 1950's, he observed, people who had lived during the cocaine "epidemic" and knew about its dangers (and that of another drug, opium – and its derivative morphine – for which addiction peaked in the 1890's but declined by 1914) had passed from the scene. The infamous reputation of cocaine also expired.[17] Because of the "loss of memory" of national drug problems, notably cocaine, in an earlier era, the nation was "condemned" to repeat history. If this information had been included as part of basic United States history, illegal drug use might not have gained a large foothold on society in the 1960's. Therefore, one area to consider as a part of school curriculum is the history of drug abuse in the nation, Dr. Musto suggested. It has not been encouraged to date in the nation's "War on Drugs" education and prevention efforts.[18]

Another lesson that appears to be connected with the need for consistent public education and prevention efforts is the importance of sustaining scientific research investigating the health aspects of drug abuse and addiction. The response of the upblic health community through NIDA's media-cocaine-prevention campaign, which eventually was extended in 1988 to include crack cocaine, was based on scientific research results (see Appendix 1). Federal research to examine the impact of cocaine in all its forms of administration, and all other illicit drugs on health, as well as keeping the public informed about these and other scientific developments could only help reduce demand for these drugs.

A component that is missing from most drug abuse prevention and addiction treatment strategies, according to NIDA Director Alan Leshner, is an emphasis on the health aspects of the drug abuse issue. He has stated that results of recent scientific research have revealed that drug addiction is "a chronic, relapsing brain disease," and therefore, a "biobehavioral disorder." Researchers have found distinct structural and functional differences between drug-addicted and normal brains at the molecular and cellular

---

[15] Ibid.

[16] Ibid., 64.

[17] Ibid.

[18] David F. Musto, telephone conversation with the author, 15 April 1998.

levels.[19] Dr. Leshner suggested that a "whole-person treatment" comprising biology, behavior, and social context," which recognizes addiction as a biobehavioral disorder, should be considered.[20] "The Great Disconnect," he contended, between ideology and science impedes formulating more effective national policies in prevention and treatment of drug abuse addiction.[21] He would like science, he explained further, to be the foundation for decisions related to drug abuse prevention and treatment. He suggested approaching the problem as a health issue instead of solely a law enforcement issue. He clarified his belief by stating,

> I believe drugs should be illegal, and I believe that we should seize them at the border. But I also believe we need to treat drug abuse or addiction as a health issue, as well. And the problem is, we've missed that part in most of our strategies. Now we have to increase its role.[22]

Dr. Leshner's comment raises the "law enforcement versus prevention" question concerning drug abuse control strategies. "Stated simply, should more emphasis be placed on punishing drug traffickers and drug users or should the public health approach of monitoring and educating the public be used to deter or reduce drug markets before they become prominent?" According to the Office of National Drug Control Policy, "The most effective strategies for preventing drug use, keeping drugs out of neighborhoods and schools, and providing a safe and secure environment for all people are cooperative efforts that mobilize and involve all elements of a community."[23] That method was used successfully in 1993 in Oahu, Hawaii, to curb the spread of "ice" a smokable form of crystal methamphetamine (popularly known as "speed").[24] The public health approach of defining the problem, identifying its causes, and developing and testing prevention programs was used by local and national law enforcement officers, local and national public health agencies, the local education department, and parents working together to discourage a drug abuse problem in Oahu.[25]

---

[19] "The NIDA Boss Touts Addiction Studies," *The Scientist: The Newspaper for the Life Sciences Professional*, 12,3 (February 2, 1998): 1.

[20] Ibid.

[21] Ibid.

[22] Ibid., 3.

[23] Office of National Drug Control Policy, "Prevention and Education," [http://www.whitehouse drugpolicy.gov/prevent/prevent.html]. No date.

[24] Marcia R. Chaiken, "The Rise of Crack and Ice: Experiences in Three Locales," *National Institute of Justice: Research in Brief*, NCJ 139559, March 1993, 1.

[25] Ibid., 6.

The procedure followed included early detection and recognition of distinct drug patterns. The local police coordinated efforts to learn about local "ice" use. The information they obtained was shared among narcotics officers, parents, teachers, other police officers involved in prevention programs, and drug abuse treatment staff. Drug prevention programs were organized by the U.S. Attorney General and the Honolulu Police Department, who worked with the Hawaii Departments of Education and Health and private organizations. To trace the drug networks importing 'ice" into the state and nation, the Honolulu police created a "crystal ball" task force and worked with federal agencies and narcotic officers in various Asian countries. Also, several agencies joined forces to pinpoint adolescent and adult "ice" users and provided effective drug treatment. Furthermore, the agencies' staff worked with school counselors and created a crystal/cocaine hotline to assist drug users. Finally, NIDA researchers were invited to field investigations and recommend better ways to monitor drug patterns. Their suggestions led to the creation of a Hawaii State Epidemiology Work Group, which initiated a more consistent way to analyze data about various drugs used by clients before being admitted to treatment programs, and a more extensive distribution of drug use survey results.[26]

The experience led some of the participants in the Hawaii effort and others (researchers, federal agency policymakers, drug abuse professionals and researchers in Oahu, as well as in Manhattan and Los Angeles where crack abuse was uncontained) to recommend a course of action that could be pursued by local area officials and community leader nationwide to reduce all forms of substance abuse, and particularly, to avert a major drug crisis through community cooperation. Their approach was to:[27]

- Form a coalition of professionals and researchers to meet and exchange relevant information regularly on any drug gaining local popularity;
- Find as many facts as possible about the properties of the drug, the method of distribution, and the appeal to users before tacking action;
- Publicize factual information about symptoms of a drug's use and its health hazards to discourage initial use. Target publicity especially at groups most likely to fine the drug appealing.

---

[26] Ibid.
[27] Ibid.

- Be alert to initial indicators of drug marketing and act rapidly to disrupt organizations simultaneously at all levels of dealing; and
- Mount a coordinated effort to identify frequent users and provide effective intervention.

This approach may be of interest to Congress as it considers ways to successfully control future nationwide outbreaks of illegal drug abuse.

Some questions remain, however, pertaining to two of the examples mentioned above that could be drawn from the crack cocaine problem – using the media's influence to deter drug use and abuse through public education programs, and the cooperative efforts used by law enforcement and public health officials to contain the spread of "ice" abuse in Hawaii.

One media-related question is, if the practice of ongoing public service announcements relating anti-drug-abuse messages were adopted, would the media be conveying mixed messages by, as some charge,[28] simultaneously subtly promoting illicit drug use through certain movies or music television videos? Media based efforts to maintain public awareness about the harmful health and social consequences of drug use and/or abuse could be diluted by other popular media presentations.

Some commentators are concerned that the glamorization of drugs, particularly cocaine, has resurfaced, if in fact it ever completely disappeared after its popularity in the 1980s.[29] "Not surprisingly," one report stated, "the Hollywood grapevine is bursting with stories about performers who have taken up cocaine, mostly those under 35 who are too young to recall Hollywood's last coke epidemic (a time when the drug was so widely used it was rumored to be factored into film budgets).[30] Such reports lead some to emphasize the need for onoing public education programs about the arguments for adding the history of past U.S. drug "epidemics" and their outcomes to school curriculums.

A question that emerges regarding the cooperative approach that successfully addressed the spread of "ice" in Hawaii is to what extent did unique circumstances or characteristics influence the effectiveness of that approach? For example, Chicago, Miami, and New York City differ

---

[28] Jeff Gordinier, "High Anxiety: As the Smoke From Recent Drug Tragedies Lingers, Why Are Movies Now Going To Pot?" *Entertainment Weekly*, 30 January 1998, 11 (Lexis-Nexis): Donna Shalala, "Media Literacy: Substance Abuse Prevention Strategy," *Current Health* 2, 23 (November 1996): S1.

[29] Dana Kennedy, "The Days of Wine and Noses: Everything Old is New Again on the Hollywood Drug Scene," *Entertainment Weekly*, 9 January 1998, 14 (Lexis-Nexis).

[30] Ibid.

substantially from Hawaii in population, size, ease of access and the demographic attributes of the populations.

Congress may decide to examine the importance of such factors in determining what combination of approaches is likely to be most effective.

APPENDIX 1: SCIENTIFIC RESEARCH ON COCAINE AND SMOKABLE COCAINE CONDUCTED IN THE 1970S

SCIENTIFIC RESEARCH ON COCAINE AND SMOKABLE COCAINE CONDUCTED IN THE 1970S

In the 1970s, powder cocaine use began to gain popularity in the United States. That situation helped stimulate scientific research, which began around 1974. Various scientists in the nation commenced analyzing the effects of cocaine use on animals and humans.[1] Controlled experiments[2] on animals and humans were performed. Preclinical animal studies were done to examine theoretical models of psychosis and to study medical uses of cocaine. Through clinical studies involving humans, negative effects of the drug and treatment results were recorded, as well as surveys and sociological reports taken regarding illicit drug use.[3] Most researchers studied the effects of the typical patterns of cocaine use in the United States, i.e., snorting cocaine powder intranasally, or injecting cocaine intravenously (IV). Some research was conducted on smoking coca paste, which was popular in South America but only minimally used by some individuals in the United States.

---

[1] House Select Committee, *Cocaine: A Major Drug Issue of the Seventies*, 81.

[2] Controlled experiments have been described as "The deliberate arrangement of experimental or research conditions so that observed effects can be directly traced to a known variable. This is often accomplished by exposing two like groups to identical conditions with the exception that one group is exposed to the variable being tested." John P. Sworetzky, *Psychology*, 6th ed. (Pacific Grove, CA: Brooks/Cole Publishing Company, 1997), 23.

[3] House Select Committee, *Cocaine: A Major Drug Issue of the Seventies*, 81.

Lester Grinspoon, a physician and Associate Professor of Psychiatry at Harvard Medical School, presented cocaine research results in his written testimony at a 1979 hearing before the House Select Committee on Narcotics Abuse and Control held to examine cocaine abuse. He found that animal experiments and some human cases showed that cocaine had a potential for abuse.[4] Results of Dr. Ronald Siegel's work, he reported, indicated that intranasal use of cocaine no more than two or three times per week, created no serious problems. Daily dosages in fairly large amounts, however, could disrupt eating and sleeping habits, produce minor psychological disturbances such as irritability and difficulty concentrating, and cause serious psychological dependence.[5] One serious outcome, Grinspoon reported, involved animals in an experiment where monkeys were given 23 hours unlimited access to intravenous cocaine. They "developed hyperactivity, tactile hallucinations, ataxia[6], severe weight loss, tremors and convulsions as they continued to inject the drug; they died within five days."[7] Grinspoon reassured Congress, however, that it was "important not to attribute to ordinary recreational use the kinds of pathological effects observed in high-dose intravenous injection by laboratory animals.[8] Investigations of the effects of coca-paste smoking on individuals were reported to the Select Committee by Robert Byck, a physician, psychiatrist, clinical pharmacologist, and Professor of Psychiatry and Pharmacology at Yale University Medical School. He recounted his involvement since 1974 in examining the effects of cocaine use and abuse on man through clinical studies. He and his Yale colleagues had conducted cocaine-related experiments in collaboration with Raul Jeri, M.D., of the University of San Marcos in Peru.

He reported that cocaine had been available in Peru for thousands of years with no known drug abuse problems until cocaine smoking emerged. The researchers discovered that individuals who smoked coca paste had greater amounts of cocaine in the blood after two minutes of smoking than after one hour in persons who used the same amount of the drug intranasally.[9] The smoking route of administration, he stated in his written testimony, appeared to have effects closer to those experienced by

---

[4] Ibid., 84.

[5] Ibid., 83.

[6] Ataxia is the "inability to coordinate the muscles in the execution of voluntary movement." *Stedman's Medical Dictionary*, 25th ed. (Baltimore: Williams & Wilkins, 1990), 147.

[7] House Select Committee, *Cocaine: A Major Drug Issue of the Seventies*, 83.

[8] Ibid.

[9] Ibid., 62.

intravenous users. "The person who smokes coca paste," he wrote, "has very intense euphoria almost immediately after he starts smoking the cigarette. Within 15 minutes after smoking one cocaine containing cigarette, his elevated mood decreases and, although he is still feeling the drug effect, he has painful anguish, depression, and drug yen. At the time of that anguish and intense drug craving, he will light up again and continue to smoke."[10] Dr. Byck emphasized the need for research to examine the dangers of smoking cocaine.

PRECLINICAL LABORATORY STUDIES ON SMOKABLE-COCAINE ABUSE

Investigations on animals into the effects of smoking cocaine freebase had been initiated nearly seven years prior to the need for such research was brought to the attention of the House Select Committee. The earliest known research that explored the impact of smokable freebase cocaine began in late 1972.[11] It was conducted by Ronald Siegel and his associates at UCLA. They performed several preclinical laboratory studies with rhesus monkeys using smokable freebase cocaine. The results were reported in the scientific literature in 1976.[12] Animal studies using the (IV) method of self-administration had been more widely performed than these oral-administration routes – chewing and/or smoking.[13]

Based on those reports, three rhesus monkeys were trained ot puff cigarettes made of cocaine freebase (0.30 grams) and lettuce (0.7 grams) placed in a commercial cigarette paper. Subsequently, the monkeys were given a choice to smoke either cocaine-lettuce cigarettes or lettuce-only cigarettes. Results, which were determined from daily one-hour sessions comparing average smoking responses (puff frequency and duration) and measuring urine levels of benzoyl ecgonine,[14] indicated that the monkeys significantly preferred the lettuce –cocaine cigarettes over the lettuce-only cigarettes.[15]

---

[10] Ibid., 91.

[11] Siegel, telephone conversation with author, 29 May 1997.

[12] Siegel, et al., "Cocaine Self-Administration in Monkeys," 461-467.

[13] Ibid., 461.

[14] Benzoyl ecgonine is a cocaine metabolite that is essential to the body's metabolizing of cocaine. Merck Index, 11th ed., 1989, 1124.

[15] Siegel et al., "Cocaine Self-Administration in Monkeys," 466.

Results of a subsequent study were published in 1980.[16] Siegel and an associate again trained three rhesus monkeys to smoke lettuce-cocaine cigarettes and monitored their urinary benzoyl ecgonine excretions, smoking responses, and changes in their overall behavior. The urinary benzoyl ecgonine excretion levels increased in all monkeys as the total number of smoked cigarettes escalated. Simultaneously, the animals' behavior was marked by hyperactivity, a rise in verbal sounds, and a decline in food intake. When the monkeys were given unlimited access to the lettuce – cocaine cigarettes, i.e., 23 hours per day over a period of 20 days, two of the three monkeys adjusted their daily intake from 5 to 5.8 cigarettes per day. Those results suggested, the researchers surmised, that "monkeys, like humans, are adjusting intake to produce desired levels of central nervous system arousal and excitation."[17]

After the experiments, Siegel observed that generally speaking, they could never find a drug that monkeys would smoke without further inducement except for cocaine freebase,[18] indicating that it seemed more addictive than others. Primates, he suggested, were good predictors of human behavior.[19] Commenting further on those results, he stated, "Like the monkeys used in the UCLA experiment, some cocaine smokers do no appear to adjust their dosage sensibly… Both the frequency and quantity of dosages escalate rapidly at freebase parties, resulting in episodes of smoking that can last from 24 to 96 hours before users become exhausted and fall asleep."[20]

Results from those experiments appeared to indicate that if humans smoked cocaine freebase, rapid addiction probably would occur.

CLINICAL STUDIES OF POSSIBLE SMOKABLE ABUSE

In 1974, the first social-recreational cocaine freebase smoking was reported in California. Consequently, the incidence of social-recreational cocaine smokers noticeably increased in the Los Angeles area. In 1975, Siegel began what became a 16-year longitudinal study of recreational use of

---

[16] Ronald Siegel and Murray E. Jarvik, "Self-regulation of Coca-Chewing and Cocaine Smoking by Monkeys," in *Cocaine 1980: Proceedings of the Interamerican Seminar on Medical and Sociological Aspects of Coca and Cocaine*, ed. F.R. Jeri, (Lima, Peru: Pacific Press, 1980).

[17] Ibid., 9.

[18] Laura Daltry, "FREEBASE: Can You Smoke Cocaine Without Getting Burnt?" *High Times*, (January 1980): 74.

[19] Siegel, telephone conversation with author, 29 May 1997.

[20] Daltry, "FREEBASE," 74, 121.

cocaine. In his letter to the editor of *The New England Journal of Medicine*, he mentioned the 1977 findings of this longitudinal study of 85 cocaine users observed that year. He noted that 14% of the participants had experimented with smoking cocaine freebase. In 1978, that percentage had grown from 14% to 39% for those who considered themselves to be primarily regular cocaine freebase smokers.[21] These users smoked freebase by placing small amounts on the burning end of a marijuana or tobacco cigarette, or by sprinkling it throughout the cigarette. About one-third gram of cocaine base was used per person when sprinkled throughout the cigarette.[22] In some instances, the cocaine freebase smokers shared one cigarette containing about one gram of freebase. The cigarette was smoked among two or three persons over an average period of four hours.[23]

Siegel noticed that patterns of use changed over a 14-year period among the social-recreational users observed in his study.[24] Dosages increased dramatically among compulsive users, Compulsive use was defined as "high frequency and high-dependency."[25] The compulsive need was primarily relatedd to wanting to induce the euphoric feelings and stimulation experienced friom initial cocaine use. Although some investigators believed compulsive cocaine users administered the drug intranasally or intravenously,[26] Siegel found in his study that compulsive users were all cocaine freebase smokers.[27]

The results of a controlled clinical laboratory investigation that compared the effects of smoking cocaine freebase with the effects experienced after an IV injection of cocaine hydrochloride appeared to corroborate Siegel's belief about compulsive cocaine users. This study was conducted by M. Perez-Reyes and his colleagues at the University of North Carolina's School of Medicine in Chapel Hill, and the Chemistry and Life Sciences Group at the North Carolina Research Triangle Institute of the Research Triangle Park.[28] Six healthy, male, paid volunteers (all recreational, predominantly intranasal, cocaine users) smoked 50 mg of cocaine freebase

---

[21] Siegel, "Cocaine Smoking," NEJM, 373.

[22] Seiegel, "Cocaine: Recreational Use and Intoxication," 125.

[23] Ibid., 126.

[24] Siegel, "Repeating Cycles of Cocaine Use and Abuse," 289.

[25] Ibid., 290.

[26] One study mentioned an overwhelming compulsion for the drug involved a study with intranasal and intravenous cocaine users conducted by Richard B. Resnick and Elaine Schuyten-Resnick, "Clinical Aspects of Cocaine: Assessment of Cocaine Abuse Behavior in Man," in *Cocaine: Chemical, Biological, Clinical, Social and Treatment Aspects*, ed. S.J. Mule (Cleveland, Ohio: CRC Press, 1976), 227.

[27] Siegel, "Repeating Cycles of Cocaine Use and Abuse," 298.

in a glass pipe under controlled smoking conditions. When inhaled, the 50 mg of freebase resulted in an intake of about 16 mg of cocaine. Two to four weeks later, the participants received a 20 mg IV dose of cocaine hydrochloride.

Researchers found that the participants had a pleasant experience and a more intense craving for the drug after smoking freebase than after the IV injection. This finding, they believed, supported the reports that drug users have a marked craving for smoking cocaine freebase. This longing leads to attempts to try and recapture the intense euphoric "high" feelings by smoking more of the drug at shorter time intervals and causes possible accumulation of cocaine in the blood. Furthermore, the investigators concluded that those results, and "the fact that smoke inhalation is a more practical way of drug use, may explain the popularity of smoking free-base cocaine."[29]

---

[28] M. Perez-Reyes et al, "Free-base Cocaine Smoking," 459-465.
[29] Ibid., 464.

APPENDIX 2: CHRONOLOGY OF EVENTS IN THE EMERGENCE OF CRACK COCAINE ABUSE IN THE UNITED STATES

EARLIEST REPORTS OF "SMOKABLE" COCAINE USE[1]

1970

- Drug dealers from California observed the smoking of cocaine base in Peru, Colombia, and Ecuador in South America. The method observed was considered very crude, because the substance smoked was coca paste. That product was derived from coca leaves dried in sulfuric acid, which condenses the alkaloids, producing a brown powder. The powder was referred to as coca paste. It differed from what eventually would become known as freebase.

- Experimental smoking of cocaine hydrochloride began in California. For example, cocaine powder was put on the end of a cigarette or sprinkled throughout a marijuana joint. Users tried several variations of this product.

---

[1] Information about the early activities related to smokable cocaine use and abuse was obtained from Siegel, "Cocaine Smoking," *JPD*, and from Witkin et al, "The Men Who Created Crack," 44 -53.

1972

- A California chemist who had heard of smoking coca paste, which was called *base* (pronounced bah-say in Spanish), accidentally discovered that the cocaine alkaloid could be freed from the hydrochloride acid salt (yielding cocaine as the "freed" base) and smoked. Upon smoking the product, he thought he was smoking "bah-say" or coca paste, but really he was smoking cocaine "freed" or freebase.[2]

- Late in the year, research scientist Ronald K. Siegel, Ph.D, and associates at the University of California, Los Angeles (UCLA) department of Pharmacology, Psychiatry, and Psychology, conducted laboratory research with three rhesus monkeys, observing how they responded to smoking cocaine freebase. The researchers noticed that the monkeys, which in past experiments had refused to smoke tobacco, had no difficulty smoking cocaine freebase.[3]

1973

- Many counterculture or "underground" press handbooks explaining how to prepare cocaine freebase were published and widely distributed in California. Those writings continued through 1976.

1974

- The first recreational cocaine freebase smoking was reported in California and was documented in the underground press.

- A 31-year-old male, admitted to the UCLA Hospital emergency room, was the first recorded person admitted for a cocaine-freebase-related problem in the United States.

---

[2] Siegel, "Cocaine Smoking," *JPD*, 288.
[3] Siegel, telephone conversation with author, 29 May 1997. Preliminary data concerning this research appeared in the *Journal of Nuclear Medicine* 15 (1974): 528. The results of the study were published as Siegel et al., "Cocaine Self-Administration in Monkeys by Chewing and Smoking," 461 – 467.

1975

- The first commercially available cocaine freebase pipes were produced in Laguna Beach, California.

- A 16-year longitudinal study of recreational cocaine users (conducted by Ronald Siegel and associates) began at UCLA using 99 social-recreational users (85 males, 14 females). Several of the subjects identified themselves as cocaine freebase smokers.[4]

1976

- Cocaine freebase smoking was first mentioned in the scientific literature (work of Siegel and others; see footnote 291).

- A book entitled *The Pleasures of Cocaine*, by Adam Gottlieb, was published in California by the underground press. It is believed to be the first book that provided a recipe for processing cocaine freebase.[5]

1977

- Cocaine freebase pipes were widely available throughout California.

- The NIDA published a report[6] about the recreational use and intoxication of cocaine. It noted the increased incidence of cocaine smoking among social-recreational users in the Los Angeles area.

1978

- In Los Angeles, a new process used to convert cocaine into a smokable form was increasing in popularity. The process was called "smearing" or "pasting." A baking soda formula was used to make

---

[4] For an overview of this study, see Siegel, "Repeating Cycles of Cocaine Use and Abuse," 289 – 320.

[5] Siegel, telephone conversation with author, 29 May 1997.

[6] Siegel, "Cocaine: Recreational Use and Intoxication," 119 – 136.

a cocaine product that would not be allowed to form into a "rock," but would be poured onto a mirror and smeared. Once dry, the drug was smoked. Some people believe that this process was the transitional product that appeared between freebase (using the volatile ether) and crack (using baking soda and water).

- Paraphernalia Headquarters of California (a drug paraphernalia industry organization) developed the first cocaine freebase extraction kits (using ether). Such kits were prepackaged groups of chemicals, glassware, and instructions for processing cocaine hydrochloride into freebase.

- The distribution of cocaine freebase pipes and extraction kits spread from California to Nevada, Colorado, New York, South Carolina, and Florida.

- An article appeared in the December 11 issue of the *San Francisco Chronicle* referring to freebase intoxication as the "ultimate high."

WARNINGS ABOUT SMOKABLE COCAINE

1979

- On January 4 - 7, the first cocaine freebase extraction kit, produced by Paraphernalia Headquarters of California, was introduced at a New York Fashion Show.

- The first national advertisements for cocaine pipes and freebase kits appeared in the January issue of *Paraphernalia Digest,* an underground-press trade journal.

- The first clinical warning about smoking cocaine appeared in the February 1979 issue of *The New England Journal of Medicine*, in a letter to the editor. It noted the growing trend of increased cocaine smoking, which was associated with the risk of dependency and toxicity. Also, it warned that "the widespread distribution and sales of cocaine pipes and other cocaine-smoking paraphernalia further signals the acceptance of the practice among social-recreational users."[7]

---

[7] Siegel, "Cocaine Smoking," *NEJM,* 373.

- The April issue of *Paraphernalia Digest* included the first "drug education bulletin" on smoking cocaine freebase.

- The May issue of the *Paraphernalia Trade Directory* indicated that wholesale distribution centers in 15 states and Puerto Rico had supplies of cocaine freebase paraphernalia.[8]

- In May, the White House Drug Policy Office requested that the Department of Justice (DOJ) consider federal legislation to prohibit the manufacture, sale, and possession of drug paraphernalia.

- The June 8 issue of the *Journal of the American Medical Association (JAMA)* included a study entitled, "Death Caused by Recreational Cocaine Use," by Drs. Charles V. Welti and Robert K. Wright of Florida's Dade County Medical Examiner's Office. They reported that since 1975, 68 deaths had been associated with the recreational use of cocaine. Therefore, they concluded that despite beliefs at the time, cocaine could not be considered a safe recreational drug.[9]

- The July issue of *Paraphernalia Digest* called cocaine freebase kits, pipes and accessories the "hottest selling line for 1979."

- In July, researchers from North and South America met in Lima, Peru, for a conference on coca and cocaine sponsored by the Pan American Health Organization and organized by the Health Department of the Ministry of the Interior of Peru. Several researchers from the United States examined Peruvian patients who were hospitalized for coca-paste smoking disorders. Observers attended from NIDA, the White House, and the Department of State.

- On July 24 and 26, the House Select Committee on Narcotics Abuse and Control held its first two-days of three hearings to examine the health consequences of cocaine. Drs. Robert C. Peterson, Assistant Director of NIDA's Division of Research, and

---

[8] Department of Health , Education and Welfare, Public Health Service, Alcohol, Drug Abuse, and Mental Health Administration, *Community and Legal Responses to Drug Paraphernalia,* by Ronald D. Wynne et al., (1980), DHEW Publication no. (ADM) 80-963, 1-62.

[9] Charles V. Welti and Robert K. Wright, "Death Caused by Recreational Cocaine Use," *JAMA,* 241(8 June 1979): 2519 – 2522.

Robert Byck of the Yale University School of Medicine both warned that smokable cocaine could be hazardous. Dr. Byck, in particular cautioned that smoking cocaine was a dangerous habit that could represent an epidemic threat to the nation.

- In August, the DEA drafted the Model Drug Paraphernalia Act in response to a request from the Whit House Drug Policy Office.

- On October 10, an additional hearing was held by the House Select Committee on Narcotics Abuse and Control to assess cocaine's impact on people's lives, and the cost of law enforcement efforts to address the cocaine problem.

- In November, two congressional hearings were held to examine the drug paraphernalia industry – on November 1, by the House Select Committee on Narcotics Abuse and Control, and on November 16, by the Senate Committee on the Judiciary's Subcommittee on Criminal Justice.

1980

- From Janusry through the end of May, several warnings about cocaine freebasing were issued in various journal and newspaper articles. Many of them were underground press publications, but some appeared also in the *Los Angeles Times, Chicago Sun Times,* and other newspapers across the nation.

- The January 16 issue of *Medical Tribune,*[10] stated that several psychiatrists reported an increase in cocaine smoking. Dr, Robert Byck is quoted as warning, "If we dont't take action now, we're going to have a huge epidemic of cocaine smoking."

- By March, it was estimated by Dr. Ronald Siegel, through analyzing available survey data from the drug paraphernalia industry, that there were about one million people in the nation who had tried smoking cocaine freebase.[11]

---

[10] Susan allport, "Epidemic of Cocaine Smoking Seen," *Medical Tribune,* (16 January 1980). Also appeared in *Hospital Tribune,* March 1980, 20.

[11] Siegel, "Cocaine Smoking," 289.

- The May 1 1980 issue of *Rolling Stone*[12] magazine included an article referring to freebase as a "treacherous obsession."

- On June 9, comedian Richard Pryor was reported to be burned accidentally, allegedly while using ether to prepare smokable cocaine freebase from cocaine powder.

- In June, NIDA issued a *NIDA Capsule*[13] about cocaine freebase, after Richard Pryor's accident, to meet the demand for information regarding this new drug practice.

THE ARRIVAL OF CRACK COCAINE

- Crack cocaine, also referred to as "rock" first appeared in Los Angeles.[14]

- The June issue of *Trade Directory*, renamed *Lifestyle Retailer Trade Directory*, published by the underground press, reported that wholesale distributors in 18 states and Puerto Rico had supplies of cocaine freebase paraphernalia.

1981

- According to the DEA, crack was first available in Los Angeles, San Diego, Houston, and Miami.

- The use of cocaine freebasing began to increase in New York City.

- By the end of the year, 23 states and several municipalities had enacted anti-drug paraphernalia legislation that was influenced by DOJ's Model Drug Paraphernalia Act.

---

[12] Charles Perry, "FREEBASE: A Treacherous Obsession," *Rolling Stone*, May 1, 1980, 42-43.
[13] National Institute on Drug Abuse, "Cocaine Freebase," *NIDA Capsules*, (June 1980): 1-2.
[14] Witkin et al., "The Men Who Created Crack." 48.

1982

- On March 5, actor/comedian John Belushi died from an overdose of a combination of cocaine and heroin.

- A 90% increase, over 1981, for cocaine overdoses was recorded in Los Angeles hospital emergency-room admissions. This near-doubling was attributed to a notable increase in cocaine users shifting from snorting to injecting to smoking.

- The street narcotics unit of the Miami Police Department raided five drug houses and apartments in Little River and Liberty City (poor neighborhoods). The houses were run by a Caribbean-island immigrant named Eliijah, who bragged to the officers that he had invented "rocks." One former officer on the scene reported that it was the first time he had seen "rocks," which also became known as crack. The raid of the drug houses and apartments was reported to be the major confirmation that crack had arrived in Miami.[15]

- "Just Say No," a slogan associated with First Lady Nancy Reagan, became what was termed a "rallying cry" for the nation to encourage drug abuse prevention among the youth.

- The Centers for Disease Control reported trends in the national surveillance of cocaine use and related health consequences in the May 28 issue of its *Morbidity and Mortality Weekly Report.*[16] Changes in the way users administered cocaine – from snorting to freebasing – were suggested to be possible reasons for an increase in the prevalence of cocaine use and adverse health consequences.

- In May, a "Cocaine Today" two-day conference was held in Los Angeles. Dr. Lee Dogoloff related the need to widely broadcast cocaine's health hazards, to change attitudes about the glamour connected with the drug's use. Drs. Ronald Siegel and David Smith (founder and medical director of the Haight-Ashbury Clinic) reported about new risks involved with cocaine freebasing. Dr. Smith reported that freebasing had increased the overall use of cocaine, which was spreading to middle-class society.

---

[15] Witkin et al., "The Men Who Created Crack." 49.

[16] "National Surveillance of Cocaine Use and Related Health Consequences," *MMWR,* 31, (28 May 1982): 265-273.

- On June 24, President Reagan declared a "War on Drugs" and created the White House Office of Drug Abuse Policy to pursue the "war."

1983

- In the early part of the year, the *Los Angeles Sentinel,* a South Central Los Angeles neighborhood community newspaper, reported the problem of "rock" houses, which were places used for dealing crack cocaine.

- On May 6, 1-800-COCAINE, a national hotline, answered its first call. The holine was begun in response to early epidemiologic data and the clinical experiences of it founders, illustrating the significant increases in cocaine use and related consequences. The hotline provided a nationwide referral service for addicts and/or their families who sought treatment or counseling, as well as, for callers, information on drug education and other available resources.

- The first 1-800-COCAINE hotline-survey of callers was conducted. It revealed that 21% of the callers were freebasing or smoking cocaine, compared with 61% abusing cocaine by snorting, and 18% injecting the drug. Sixty percent had incomes of $25,00 and less per year, while 40% made over $25,000. Eighty-five percent were white, 15% were black or Hispanic, 67% were males, 33% females, the average age was 30 years, and 1% were adolescents. [17]

- An article in the May issue of *The U.S. Journal* reported that the price of cocaine had dropped, making it increasingly available.[18]

- In December, a former Bronx, New York, narcotics policeman who directed a "street research unit" reported to have heard two drug abusers in the Tremont section of the Bronx talk about a new drug called crack and/or "rock" cocaine being used in the area.

---

[17] Herb Roehrich and Mark S. Gold. "800-COCAINE: Origin, Significance, and Findings." *The Yale Journal of Biology and Medicine,* 61 (March/April 1988): 151.

[18] Tom Seay, "White House – NIDA Differ: Purity and Availability Up ...Price Down for Heroin and Cocaine," *The U.S. Journal of Drug and Alcohol Dependence,* 7 (May 1983): 3.

1984

- As recorded by the Drug Abuse Warning Network (DAWN) of NIDA, the number of cocaine-smoking-related injuries nationwide rose from 618 to 1,274, an increase of 106%, from 1984 to 1985. Much of the increase was believed to be due to the smoking of crack, as opposed to the more traditional freebase cocaine (prepared with ether).

- Cocaine-related hospital emergency admissions nationwide, reported through DAWN, were 8,201, and there were 666 cocaine-related deaths (New York City data not included).[19]

- In June, NIDA began planning a national-media cocaine prevention campaign.

- Sales of $25 vials of "rock" swept through south central Los Angeles. A former Los Angeles police captain stated that dozens of "rock" houses seemed to appear overnight.[20]

- Crack had spread more widely to poor Miami neighborhoods, selling for as little as $10, often under such brand names as "Rambo" or "Miami Vice," according to the head of the Miami Police Department's street narcotics unit.

1985

- Cocaine-related hospital emergency admissions nationwide were 10,371, and there were 748 cocaine-related deaths (New York City data not included). [21]

- A survey of hotline calls to 1-800-COCAINE revealed that 30% of callers were freebasing – compared with 21% in the 1983 survey – 64% were white, 36% were black or Hispanic, the average age was 27 years, 7% were adolescents, 58% were males, 42% were females, and 73% had yearly incomes of $25,000 and less, while 27% made over $25,000.[22]

---

[19] Drug Enforcement Administration, *Crack Cocaine; Overview 1989,* 2.

[20] Witkin et al., "The Men Who Created Crack," 48.

[21] Drug Enforcement Administration, *Crack Cocaine: Overview 1989,* 2.

[22] Roehrich and Gold, "800-COCAINE," 149 – 155.

- The February issue of *Th U.S. Journal* announced the arrival of 'rock" cocaine in Los Angeles as a new epidemic. The phenomenon was attributed to the easy availability of what was once "the rich white man's drug." The problem appeared to be occurring only in black neighborhoods.[23]

- An article appeared in the July 5 issue of *JAMA* [24] discussing the danger of using cocaine. The author, William Pollin, the Director of NIDA, noted that there had been an intensive and destructive increase in the use of cocaine combined with other drugs among the population of cocaine users, including freebasers. Furthermore, he stated, "The really great dangers that would befall the nation, should a substantial decrease in cocaine's prices lead to a sharp increase in number of users, have recently been dramatically summarized" (he referred to a cocaine symposium update held on March 7, 1985 in New York City.)

- On July 16, the House Select Committee on Narcotics Abuse and Control held hearings to assess the problem of cocaine abuse and how the federal government should respond. Dr. Arnold Washton, of the National Hotline, testified that cocaine abuse had reached epidemic proportions and continued to escalate.[25]

- In the fall, crack trafficking was first identified in the Bronx and upper Manhattan, New York. According to the DEA, crack became a serious problem in New York City during this year.

- In October, Robert Stutman became special agent in charge of the DEA New York City office. One of the first things he heard about was crack cocaine. This occurrence was dubbed "The Feds Finally Catch On" in a 1991 *U.S. News and World Report* article.[26] Also, the article reports that the federal officials had a difficult time trying to determine how widespread the crack problem was because they could not decode the street "lingo." The confusion was said to have slowed down law enforcement response to the problem.

---

[23] Ruppert, "New Epidemic: 'Rock' Cocaine Hits L.A.," 1,4.

[24] William Pollin, "The Danger of Cocaine," *Journal of the American Medical Association,* 254 (5 July 1985): 98.

[25] House Select Committee on Narcotics Abuse and Control, *Cocaine Abuse and the Federal Response: Hearing,* 99th Cong., 1st Sess., 16 July 1985 (Washington, D.C.: U.S. Government Printing Office, 1985), 31.

[26] Witkin et al., "The Men Who Created Crack," 50.

- On November d17-19, the first national conference on cocaine entitled, "The Clinical Challenge: Cocaine," was held in New York City, cosponsored by the Regent Hospital in New York City, the Fair Oaks Hospital of Summit, New Jersey, and the 800-COCAINE National Hotline.

- Late in the year, crack was reported to be deeply rooted in poor neighborhoods in New York City and in two other cities, Los Angeles and Miami.[27]

- In November, the *New York Times* first published reports on crack cocaine abuse.[28]

- The December 31 issue of the *Atlanta Journal*, included an item entitled, "Bahamas 'Free-basing Epidemic' cited."[29] It reported a warning by Dr. David Allen, a Harvard-trained psychiatrist who headed the islands' National Drug Council, that the world's first freebasing epidemic, which he felt was being experienced in the Bahamas, had the potential of being a forerunner to a possible freebase epidemic in "the industrialized states."

INCREASED CRACK ABUSE

1986

- The January issue of *The U.S. Journal* reported highlights from the November 1985 national Cocaine Conference. Dr. Sidney Cohen, a UCLA professor in its Neuropsychiatric Institute, reported that increasing coca crops and cocaine stockpiles in South America had caused a drop in consumer costs for the drug[30] and made it plentiful.

---

[27] Los Angeles, Miami, and New York were major distribution points for cocaine. Consequently, they were the first cities to be engulfed with crack. Massing, "Crack's Destructive Sprint Across America," 58.

[28] Boundy, "Program for Cocaine-Abuse Under Way," *New York Times,* 17 November 1985, sec. 11WC, p. 12; Gross, "A New Purified Form of Cocaine Causes Alarm As Abuse Increases," *New York Times,* 29 November 1985, sec. A, p. 1.

[29] "Bahamas 'Free-basing epidemic' Cited," *The Atlantic Journal,* 31 December 1985, sec. A,p.5.

[30] Milan Korcok, "Cheap Cocaine Fueling Demand," *The U.S. Journal of Drug and Alcohol Dependence,* 10 January 1986): 16.

As a result, many people who ordinarily would not have been in the market for cocaine were spending their life savings for the drug.

- Between 1985 and 1986, DAWN reported that cocaine-smoking-related injuries increased an astonishing 296%, with more than 5,000 injuries reported in 1986. [31]

- By spring, crack was available in all areas of New York City, as well as the surrounding suburbs. It was particularly prominent in the Washington Heights neighborhood of northern Manhattan.

- The first report of a nationwide (occurring in the Bahamas) medical epidemic due to freebase cocaine abuse was published in the March 1 issue of *The Lancet,* a medical journal.[32]

- The DEA reported that crack seemed to explode on the drug scene, with reported availability in 28 states and the District of Columbia.

- Cocaine-related hospital emergency admissions nationwide, reported through DAWN, were 18,991, and there were 1,269 cocaine-related deaths (New York City data not included).[33]

- In April, NIDA launched a multimedia cocaine abuse prevention campaign called, "Cocaine: The Big Lie." The target group was 18- to 35-year-old cocaine users.

- In May, a 1-800-COCAINE survey revealed that out of 458 primary cocaine users who called, 144 (33%) were using crack. Additional information from the survey caused hotline researchers to conclude that there was an increasing incidence of crack use, distinguished by rapid addiction and significant medical problems.[34]

- On June 19, an all-day briefing was held in New York City by DEA agents and chemists, New York police, private treatment providers, officials from the Department of Justice, and NIDA discussing the crack issue.

---

[31] Drug Enforcement Administration, *Crack Cocaine Availability*, 4.

[32] James F. Jekel et al., "Epidemic Free-Base Cocaine Abuse: Case Study From the Bahamas," *The Lancet*, 1 (1 March 1986): 459-462.

[33] Drug Enforcement Administration, *Crack Cocaine: Overview 1989*, 1.

[34] Washton and Gold, "Crack," [Letter to the Editor], *JAMA*, 256 (8 August 1986): 711.

- On June 19, University of Maryland basketball star Len Bias died from a cocaine overdose.

- On June 27, Don Rogers, a defensive linebacker for the Cleveland Browns football team, died after snorting cocaine at his bachelor's party.

- On July 15, a joint hearing was held by the House Select Committee on Narcotics Abuse and Control and the Select Committee on Children, Youth, and Families. David Westrate, DEA Assistant Administrator for Operations, testified that the DEA perceived that crack had emerged as a major drug problem in less than one year. Also, there was "no comprehensive analysis of the crack problem either from a health or enforcement viewpoint."[35]

- On July 15, the Senate Permanent Subcommittee on Investigations of the Committee on Governmental Affairs held hearings to examine the concerns about crack cocaine. Dr. Robert Byck of the Yale University Medical School testified. He mentioned his 1979 testimony before the House Select Committee on Narcotics Abuse and Control and the warning he had given about a potential national problem with cocaine freebase, which he felt had gone unheeded.[36]

- On July 18, the House Select Committee on Narcotics Abuse and Control held a hearing in New York City to examine crack cocaine use, which was believed to be widely spread throughout the City.[37]

- In August, a letter to the editor appeared in *JAMA* from 1-800-COCAINE surveyors.[38] They noted the urgent need to inform the medical community about the crack problem, and stated that, to their knowledge, no reports about the abuse had yet appeared in the medical literature. Also, they warned that the strong appeal of crack to users and dealers indicated that its popularity would continue to grow.

---

[35] House Select Committee on Narcotics Abuse and Control and the Select Committee on Children, Youth, and Families, *The Crack Cocaine Crisis, Joint Hearing*, 149, 158.

[36] Senate Committee on Governmental Affairs, Senate Permanent Subcommittee on Investigations, *"'Crack Cocaine'," Hearing*, 99th Cong., 2nd sess., 15 July 1986, 19.

[37] House Select Committee on Narcotics Abuse and Control, *Trafficking and Abuse of "Crack" in New York City, Hearing*, 99th Cong. 2nd sess., 18 July 1986, 117.

[38] Washton and Gold, "Crack", 711.

- A DEA report, published in September, stated that crack was considered to be a secondary rather than a primary problem in most areas where it was available.[39]

- By fall, the 1-800-COCAINE hotline personnel estimated that one million Americans had tried crack, in large part because the drug's marketing structure was changing and distribution was expanding.[40]

- On September 8, legislation (H.R. 5484) was introduced in Congress to authorize various federal programs to combat illicit drug trafficking and drug abuse.

- On September 14, President Reagan and the First Lady spoke against the drug abuse "menace," especially crack cocaine, during a nationally televised broadcast.

- On September 15, President Reagan submitted to Congress the "Drug-Free America Act of 1986" requesting immediate consideration and enactment of the legislation which he hoped would become the cornerstone of the Administration's antidrug efforts.

- On October 3, the House Select Committee on Narcotics Abuse and Control held hearings in conjunction with the Congressional Black Caucus to examine the federal response to drug trafficking and abuse.

- On October 27, H.R. 5484, the Anti-Drug Abuse Act of 1986 became Public Law 99-570. H.R. 1625, the "Mail Order drug Paraphernalia Control Act of 1986." Was inserted into Title 1 of the law, "Anti-Drug Enforcement," as Subtitle O, "Prohibition on the Interstate Sale and Transportation of Drug Paraphernalia."

1987

- According to DEA data, crack was available in 46 states and the District of Columbia.

---

[39] Drug Enforcement Administration, *The Crack Situation in the United States*, 1-45.

[40] Witkin et al., "The Men Who Created Crack," 51.

- On February 26, the House Select Committee on Narcotics Abuse and Control held a hearing to assess the status of federal drug abuse education and treatment programs created in schools under the Anti-Drug Abuse Act of 1986.

- On March 11, the House Select Committee on Narcotics Abuse and Control held hearings to review the Alcohol, Drug Abuse and Mental Health Administration's progress in implementing federal aid to states for drug abuse treatment and prevention programs under the Anti-Drug Abuse Act of 1986.

- During the first 8 months of the year, for the first time, cocaine-smoking-related hospital admissions surpassed those involving injection and snorting.

- DAWN and other state and public health organizations reported dramatic increases over previous years in the number of crack-cocaine-related deaths, emergency room admissions, and treatment facility visits.

- Projected crack-cocaine-related injuries showed 114% increase over the 1986 total.[41]

- On March 26, President Reagan created the National Drug Policy Board by Executive Order 12590. The board was directed to facilitate and coordinate the national drug policy, and integrate activities of Executive departments and agencies to address the illegal drug abuse problem.

1988

The DEA reported that crack was available in almost every state in the union, and was considered to be a major medical problem.

Forty-nine states and the District of Columbia had sought to control the sale of drug paraphernalia through state laws or local ordinances. Furthermore, 39 of those states and DC enacted statutes based on the DEA Model Drug Paraphernalia Act. Through those actions, the drug paraphernalia industry was basically legislated out of existence or at least driven underground.

---

[41] Drug Enforcement Administration, *Crack Cocaine Availability*, 4.

The last phase of NIDA's "Cocaine:The Big Lie" campaign began and was designed to address crack-abusing teenagers and assist families of cocaine abusers.

For the first time in over 10 years, the University of Michigan's National High School Seniors Survey reported, cocaine use among high school seniors had declined.[42]

In March, the White House held a national "Drug-Free America" conference, at which First Lady Nancy Reagan stated that the casual drug user must be discouraged from abusing drugs as much as the drug addict.[43]

On November 18, the Anti-Drug abuse act of 1988 became Public Law 100-690. It created the Office of National Drug Abuse Control Policy to develop policies, precedences, and goals for the national drug control program.

---

[42] Charles Culhane, "First Drop in Decade: Cocaine Use Slacks Off in High Schools," *The Journal of Drug and Alcohol Dependence,* 12 (February 1988): 1.

[43] Charles Culhane, "White House Conference; First Lady Blasts 'Casual' Users," *The U.S. Journal of Drug and Alcohol Dependence,* 12 (April 1988): 1.

INDEX